GHOSTS OF AMERICA 6.
rights reserved. No part of this l
any manner whatsoever withou
case of brief quotations embodi
For information visit our website www.ghostsofamerica.com.

In order to protect the privacy of the people that have submitted stories some names and locations have been left out.

All stories were originally submitted by our audience to ghostsofamerica.com. The stories have been edited by us to better fit this book.

Compiled and edited by: Nina Lautner

Acknowledgements

We would like to thank all those who have submitted their stories to us. These are the people who make our site ghostsofamerica.com and this book possible.

We would also like to thank all the lost souls in these stories. We hope many of them will have found their way by the time this book is published.

CONTENTS

1.

Stay Clear

Edgemoor, South Carolina

I was raised in my great aunt's house which was built in 1908. Two of my three aunts died in the home. The house is on Edgeland Road in Edgemoor. I am forty-seven now, but as a child my parents raised my sister, brother, and myself in this house. From the age of four to sixteen I lived in fear. There was always a feeling of being watched, and I always slept in a small bed beside my parents. One night I awoke and was trying to go back to sleep. I began feeling weight at the end of the bed, and I could feel the mattress press down. It began to move up toward me like someone was crawling into bed with me. We had cats, and I thought one had jumped on the bed, so I raised up to make it get down. When I looked there was nothing there, and the presence was gone. I always got up early, and my mother would have breakfast started every morning before I ever got up.

There was one night I slept in the second bedroom, and when I awoke I heard pans being moved in the kitchen. I got up and walked through the house to the kitchen which was on the other end of the house. I walked into the den which was right before the kitchen door, and the kitchen light was on. I heard the sound of a pan being moved. When I walked through the kitchen door I began to say good morning to my mother, but she was not there. I looked in the mud room next to the kitchen, and she was not there either. I noticed a pan on the stove, but the stove was not on. I got scared and went to find my mother. When I found her she was sound asleep in the bed with my father. I began to scream and like always they told me I must have just imagined everything. That was when I knew it was useless to say anything about what was happening to me.

We moved to a new home when I was in the 11th grade, and it just became a nightmare I wanted to forget. Time makes things seem less important because I later acquired the home after my grandparents had passed away. It was a terrible mistake to move back into the house because as an adult things went from a small haunting to something totally different. As a child I never experienced things being moved or hearing voices of any kind. I had met a girl who later moved in with me. The relationship was great at first like most relationships but soon changed. She acknowledged that she had seen a black form come from the dining room into the den where she was sitting. I knew she believed in astrology, but I did not know until later she was into witchcraft. She had gotten this belief from her mother, and I did not like it at all. It made me angry towards her because I believe in god and I wanted no part of it.

Time went on, and things were bad. When I was in the bathroom one day I noticed a burn which had gone through the tile to the wood on the bathroom floor beside the tub. She had put the bath mat over it hoping I would not notice it. I asked her about it, and she was burning a charcoal in a glass ashtray while quoting some witch spell to rid the house of bad spirits. Evidently something must have scared the hell out of her. I was mad because she almost caught the house on fire, and I knew she had to go. When she left I began to have huge paintings fly off the wall at night. Water would come on by itself in that same bathroom sink. One night I came in late, and some weird deep voice said "welcome home" as I stepped into the front door. I knew I was not hearing things because my dog in the house started going crazy. My dog started acting weird and barking into rooms that no one was in. I could hear the springs moving on my grandfather's bed like it did when I got into it at night, but I was in the other room!

One night I heard a cough right beside me, and I thought someone was in my home. My dog also barked when this happened. I found no one in the house. Lights began cutting on by themselves, and a touch lamp in the den one night went from low medium to high all by itself. My dog began to stay sick, and the vet could find nothing wrong and said it seemed like a nervous disorder of some kind. I finally had enough and just abandoned the house because my luck seemed to be always bad with one problem after another. I knew the house was haunted, but I think my witch girlfriend had brought something in a lot worse. Some people from New York got the house later on, and I warned the wife the house was haunted. She told me she liked the idea of having a ghost. I thought she would eat those words sooner than later. I notice they have not been there too many years, and they now have it up for sale. I wonder why? Everyone should stay clear of this house if you have kids, or I promise that you will regret it. I have lived and stayed in a lot of places in my life and have never had this kind of problem anywhere else. I do not care if you believe, but whoever stays in that house long enough will!

Submitted by Chuck, Edgemoor, South Carolina

. . . .

2.

After Grandmother Moved In
Wappingers Falls, New York

My family moved to Wappingers when I was around ten. My dad was a steamfitter at the time at Indian Point, and my mom was a stay at home. We bought a house on Brothers Road and moved up from West Haverstraw. It was a nice old ranch house. My bedroom was right above the garage. My grandmother was quite ill, and my father being the awesome son built an addition on our house to move her out of a nursing home and into our house where he said she belonged.

To this point in my memory there was nothing strange; it was after my grandmother had to move back into a facility that things got crazy. My folks got divorced, and my brother and I continued to live with my mother in that same house. It was around that time things got sketchy.

There were two rather large windows off the kitchen, and on them hung those ornaments that were made in the early 1980s by melting plastic beads into lead frames in the oven. Anyway, you could not make it from one end of the house to the other without those things banging away on the glass. Even the dog would make them rattle but never the wind. One day my brother and I were sitting in the "family" room. We were alone like many of the latch key kids of the day when we heard the creaking of the floor and the ornaments clanging against the glass. I leaned my head back in typical teenage prose and hollered "YO. " I heard nothing in reply. The dog was with us... Hmm. I got up and walked out to see if maybe my mother had come home early, no dice, nobody anywhere in the house. On the way back to the TV, I noticed that the ornaments were still moving. I froze thinking it was me. That is when the hanging lamp started to swing from side to side. I could not speak, with tears running down my face; I went and got my brother and we went outside until my mother got home. At first she did not believe me. Then it got worse.

There were always footsteps, audible and those damn ornaments always clanging away, but the most interesting event happened not too much later and that caught my mother's attention, and made me look for a new place to live!

My father had stopped by to get my brother and I for a camping trip. As he waited in the door for us to gather our gear, there was a horrible loud and offensive tearing noise. I cannot even begin to describe it to this day. My dad being the protector busted into the house and ran into where he thought the noise came from which was my mother's dining room. Remember that addition that we built for grandma, well the upstairs was for us, and my mother wanted her dining room. Along the longest wall was a very large buffet table, and above that was the largest mirror known to man; maybe an exaggeration but it was huge, nonetheless. I can vividly remember my father installing this mirror. He was never one to under engineer anything, and he pounded giant five- inch spikes into the wall into the studs that he had intentionally added for this very purpose. Three of these gigantic iron spikes and they were in turn wired together to distribute the load I was told. Back to the big event. That mirror, that giant framed piece of glass that must have weighed over 100 pounds had been pulled down, not off, just down. Above the frame was a huge horrific gash in the sheetrock with shards of wood pulled out from the studs behind. The mirror now sat balanced on the stacks of mother's finest china plates. Not one was cracked.

We left in great haste. Before the advent of cell phones, my mother had to wait until our return on Sunday to hear the explanation, much to her disbelief. In that same house I have watched coffee cups slide off the table, been held down in my bed, and awakened too just as fast, and once to protect my brother from falling down the stairs. One night in the midst of all of these

10

events, I woke up at around 3:00 am for no reason. There was full moon; it shined through my window brightly. As I tossed to fall asleep again, I looked out the window and was frozen in fear. Out on the street a full sized figure, all white and hazy was staring back at me. I tried to scream out but could not move any air. As I watched this figure, it turned and began its way down the street away from the house until it simply vanished. It was a full moon, and no trees were blocking my view. To this day when I visit that house I can still tell you exactly where that apparition was.

Wappingers has a strange history for sure. I have lived in Maine since 1996 only visiting once or twice a year when possible. My mother still lives in that same house. She must have made her peace with whatever was there...or...

Submitted by Bob, Wappingers Falls, New York

. . . .

3.

Don't Drive Tired

Baraboo, Wisconsin

I was living south of Madison and dating a gal who was living in Baraboo and frequently making late night trips. I got done with work one evening and headed north on Hwy 12 to go visit, as I had many times before. I was pretty drowsy as it was around "bar time"(2-3 AM), so I was a little freaked out by a guy walking down the road. I remember thinking "Wow, that idiot is going to get whacked by some drunk driver. "

So far as I can recall, this was next to the airport on the right (east) side of the road. The guy walking had a green vest, greasy black hair, a hat, (or ball cap-ish) and blue jeans. I think he had some sort of flannel under the vest because the (darker than the OD green vest) sleeves showed dark contrast. He was walking north "with traffic" on the right side of the road.

After the initial charge of alertness was wearing off, I was further up the road. I passed through the intersection and was passing the cemetery on the north east corner of that intersection (if anyone has travelled the road, where I am describing should be pretty clear) when I could see someone walking further up the road. Now, this was after the cemetery, but before the "S" turn before the trailer park and gas station area on the west (left) side of the road. As I got closer, I identified a pedestrian and changed to the left lane to give them room. It was cold, and I did not want to blast them with the wind as I passed.

The closer I got, the clearer it was that it was THE SAME GUY with OD green vest, jeans, darker long-sleeved sleeved shirt, ball-cap sort of hat, shiny (greasy looking) shoulder length black hair. He had the same height and same build; the stride was even the same. Of course, I was freaked out for the rest of the trip. WIDE AWAKE NOW! Wow, I could not figure it out. I am a pretty scientific observer from military training and other endeavors, so this incident had me mystified. I feel compelled to offer the best report as I am able. I was a bartender, and yes, I had a shift drink but was far from drunk. I was tired; that is true. However, to see something once then have it repeated? I cannot deny seeing what I saw. I looked closely the second time. My eyes and sight were clear. The weather was clear. There were no headlights behind me, no tail lights in front of me, and no other traffic oncoming or potential light inputs of any sort besides the headlights of my car. I cannot discount what I saw as a glare or freak light trick. There was not even a cop running radar in the median (trust me, I was looking. That stretch is notorious for speed traps, and it was that magical time of the night when the drunks are out.)

I put it out of my head unresolved as a "freaky thing. " Several weeks later, the gal I was seeing started up a conversation regarding interesting "haunted" places locally and loaded a website to show me. After describing the downtown Baraboo bar and reading an article, she announced the title of the next article to discuss would be Highway 12 Hitchhiker. "Wait, wait. Vest, black hair, cap, jeans, walking. I saw him twice - once, then once later further up the road. Unprovoked and having never heard of the "story," what I experienced fit the description.

I would love to say that two pranksters dressed up the same and perpetuated a hoax. If they did, good job, but why would they be walking up and down a stretch of desolated stretch of road in the middle of the night? Trying to get killed? No, it was THE SAME PERSON. You cannot fake a stride. These "two" walked the same way. Hair was even styled the same. I cannot confirm a beard, though, as I was coming up from behind, and the headlights did not light up behind me to show the face as I passed.

The theory I came up with is that I probably would have fallen asleep at the wheel and, well, died? I hit and killed a pedestrian? Whatever, something terrible, and this "spirit" or whatever you would like to refer to was waking me up. Thanks, hitcher. I do not drive tired anymore, message received. I imagine that he is walking that road waking people up, so they do not kill someone like he got killed. I am afraid that, even if I was to research news articles to try and find a match, whichever drunk that hit the guy probably just rode off into the night thinking they hit a deer. Odds are that the accident was never reported, and the guy's body was dragged off by coyotes, and his soul is left to wander without the closure of a burial.

If you want to see the Highway 12 Hitcher, drive tired at bar time up that stretch. Better yet, DON'T drive tired. You might kill someone.

Submitted by SB, Baraboo, Wisconsin

. . . .

4.

The Farmer

Derby, Connecticut

In the almost fifty years I have been on this earth I have lived in several haunted houses. For now I will tell you about one of them. Although this house was not the worst it still made me and my (non-believing) husband sit up and take notice. It was in December when twenty-five years ago I moved into our newly rented old fourteen-room house (built in the late 17th century) on Rosseter Street in Great Barrington, MA. We felt like we had hit the lottery, but it had a few seriously nasty inhabitants in residence as we found out. The occurrences started the very night we moved in with at that time our three small children. After putting the children to bed my husband and I were sitting in the living room on the couch relaxing after a long day. We heard heavy furniture being moved around upstairs. We had moved from a tiny apartment, and all of our things including all of us fit into just the downstairs with plenty of room left over.

My husband insisted it was our dog tied on the porch dragging her dog chain as she went up and down the steps. I pointed out to him the dog was sleeping on the floor right next to the couch we were sitting on. He went upstairs to investigate, only to return saying there was indeed nothing but dust bunnies up there. Several times my oldest (five-year-old) would wake in the middle of the night terrified because there was a man with "bugs" crawling out of his face sitting on his dresser. Frequently my two-year-old would play with a "friend" while his two older siblings were in daycare. He said he was playing with his new friend, and her name was Alexandria (who lived in his bedroom) when I questioned him. Then one night there was a bad wind storm, and our outside pantry door flew open with a loud bang. My husband got up out of bed to close it. When he returned he asked me who I let in the front door. He had seen a tall man dressed in black with a black hat standing in the front hall. I told him I had let no one in the

15

front door. I had not gotten out of bed. He was so insistent that a man had been standing there. He searched the house up and down to find no one.

That summer when my dog had puppies she was insistent on placing one of the four she gave birth to in my lap while she delivered the others. They were all healthy puppies, but that one (that she kept getting up to place in my lap) was the only one to survive. The other three died within a week in that house. Plants and spiders did not even live there! We would hear all kinds of things, voices, things moving on their own or missing, only to turn up in places we had just checked previously. One day while I was in the attic I discovered a hidden room by the top of the stairs by accident. Up until that moment I believed it was just a wall. Inside I discovered a pair of old long-johns with wooden buttons down the front and on the back flap, as well as a newspaper dated 1783 (it has been a long time so I am not too clear on the last two numbers). They both were in perfect condition. In that paper was a short article discussing a certain young girl's death and things about her father. Time went on, and we were always seeing flashes of people walking around out of the corner of our eyes.

The cellar terrified me the most even when another person was with me. The first time we went into the cellar to look around we saw an old room built into the back corner. It used to be an old coal chute. God only knows the last time it had been used and was boarded up from the outside. We decided it would be a good place to store some things. We went down with arms loaded to make our deposit to discover the room was no longer there! The final straw came when I was eight months pregnant with my last child. I was bringing towels from one of the upstairs bathrooms to the one downstairs. As I started to descend the stairs getting about three steps down something or someone pushed me hard from behind! The towels went flying to the bottom of the stairs, and I just managed to catch myself from falling by grabbing the banister with both hands. At the time all three of my children were

16

sound asleep napping in their downstairs bedroom, and my husband was at work.

The next day I went and researched the house's history. I found it was one of the first houses to be built in Great Barrington. It was built by a wealthy farmer, and at that time it was a very large farm taking up most of the land that is now downtown. He was not what you would call a nice man in life and had a young daughter who died in the house under questionable circumstances. Her name was Alexandria. The same girl the old news paper article spoke of. The same girl my little son played with. We eventually moved out of that house, and it has since been torn down. Another smaller one story house was built there, but you can still feel the presence on the property when you drive or walk by.

Submitted by Karen, Derby, Connecticut
. . . .

5.

Behind The Iron Gate

Denison, Texas

There was an old boarded up house out at the end of River Oaks Road east of Denison with a huge iron gate. The house was accompanied by a smaller trailer home on the same property and surrounded by woods that backed right up to the Red River. No one used the property, and it was virtually abandoned, though sometimes we would see people go in and out of the gate. This house and the trailer both, and most likely the land itself, is HIGHLY haunted. I personally, along with several other people from the neighborhood witnessed apparitions moving through the house, screams coming from the house and the trailer, and horrible smelling odors wafting through the air if you got too close. As a teenager, a friend and I decided to "investigate" the house and trailer in broad daylight. Mind you we were met with unspeakable horrors.

The trailer which we ventured into first was filled with trash and what looked to be human waste covering the walls, ceilings, and floors, as if someone had been throwing it around. As we stepped inside, pieces of trash started to lift off of the floor as we watched and came flying at our heads. We took off of course and never went back. However, we did return and go into the large two-story house. The door was locked, so we managed to find a window that was unlocked, and shimmied inside. Inside the house we found that it had been abandoned mid-construction. The framing was up but nothing else. There were, however, random pieces of furniture here and there, and the kitchen had all of its appliances. Again, we were there in broad daylight, and the entire place felt extremely dead. It was as if the air in the house were a thousand years old.

Walking through the house, we continued to hear what sounded like footsteps above us on the second floor and groaning sounds.

When the sounds were investigated, there was no one there. There were, however, letters strewn about the house, all of them "get well soon" and "sorry for your loss" cards. It seemed creepy, really creepy, but not malicious like the trailer had been. Being the know-it-all adventure seeking teen that I was, I returned to the house again with a couple of friends several weeks later, this time at night. The friend who had been with me the first time refused to enter the house. He said it just felt "really dark". The other friend and I entered and did not stay long. As we were moving through the house, we noticed that we could not see anything. Even though there was a bright moon out, and we had a flashlight, it was like there was a heavy fog around us blocking all light inside the house. Then as we were standing there, it got freezing cold. It was so cold we started to shiver. I felt something grab me by the hair and pull me away from my friend. I screamed, ran, and grabbed my friend. We ran out the door. As we crossed the threshold of the door, the door slammed behind us, and we could hear the lock click.

We ran away from the house, and the girl that had stayed outside the whole time was standing about 100 yards away and was just standing completely still. She was staring up at the second story balcony. We turned, looked up, and saw a huge black figure. He was as tall if not taller than the glass door behind it. It was only a shadow figure. As we were watching, it hissed something at us and turned and walked through -- THROUGH!-- the closed door and back into the pitch black. We never went back.

Several years later, I visited my father who still lived on that street. One day a truck took the corner too fast and got stuck in our drain ditch. I went out to help them get it unstuck, and I started talking to the elderly woman who had been driving. It turned out she was the woman who owned the property. She lived in California and was here on "family business. " She told me that they were finally going to tear the house down. I casually asked her what the story was behind the house. She told me that before

19

her husband died, they had moved here with their son and daughter-in-law. They all stayed in that trailer while building the house. All she said was that the daughter-in-law and the son had both died in the trailer. After the funeral, when construction on the house resumed, her husband had an "accident" in the house and died. She left the house unfinished and moved away.

That is all I know. The house is now gone, but people still hear screams from behind the huge iron gate that remains across the driveway.

Submitted by Corrie, Denison, Texas

. . . .

6.

Just Checking

Somerville, Massachusetts

In November 1970 I lived in an old four-flat rental house on Springfield Street just off Cambridge Avenue near Inman Square in Somerville. I had the middle bedroom of three in a row. It was right off the kitchen, and two other roommates shared the apartment. I was awakened one night by feeling my bed bounce. As I looked up, I saw a black dog jump off the foot of my bed. I presumed I was dreaming, and I then got up to go to the bathroom. I went right back to bed and tried to fall asleep again. I soon heard the front door of the apartment open followed by the sound of footsteps.

I assumed it was one of my roommates coming back from a night out. As I lay in bed listening to the approaching footsteps, I was seized with an overwhelming fear and paralysis. I looked at the open doorway to my room and saw a human shaped figure approach my bed. This entity was short and had a huge round head. It came to my bedside and leaned on the side of my bed (and the mattress moved accordingly) and looked at me lying there.

I felt real terror and could feel my heart racing, but I could not move. In a moment it was gone, and I could close my eyes and take a breath again. I told no one about this. About a month later, I was sleeping in bed with my future husband when I was awakened by a noise he was making. It sounded like he was trying to speak or scream, but he seemed unable to move his mouth. I thought he was having a nightmare, so I gently touched him and tried to waken him. When I roused him he said he was awake, but he had become frightened and paralyzed by an apparition that approached him in bed and leaned over him and stared at him. He was trying to alert me, but he could not move. The next day I told him about my experience. We decided that whatever the entity was it was perhaps just checking us and making its presence known. We had no further visits while we lived on Springfield Street, and we moved to California soon thereafter. The building was later torn down and is now a parking lot.

Submitted by Chris, Somerville, Massachusetts

. . . .

7.

The Creature

Upton, Massachusetts

One night in the year of 2014 I was walking along Christian Hill Road in Upton. It was bitterly cold, and the wind crawled across my face. It was January, and the road had just been plowed of this particular hour, around one am. I had originally gone for a walk to clear my head. However, as my body adapted to the single digit temperature and the whipping winds, I found myself just sort of lumbering around and singing local band melodies.

I then came to a cease in my aimless traipse and sat on a log in front of the fields shivering. I was not inebriated or hallucinatory in any manner, but when I saw the figure I thought for a second I might be. It was tall and skinny, and it wore what seemed like a brightly colored raiment, but in the thick darkness the cloth looked pale with only hints of blue and green. At first I had the supposition that the figure was a rather tall man that lived in the RV off of the road for there are a few homeless people that roam about Upton, as some of the other stories on this site have accounted for. As I observed the figure steadily, for I do not believe he saw me at that point, I noted his erratic and even fatuous behavior. For what seemed like a solid ten minutes it dug in the snow with its bare hands and bent over the entire time like it had just leaned over to touch its toes. When it snapped back upwards its long black hair flipped up and behind its head, as it had been hanging down in its face. It lifted its hands in the air and then collapsed them immediately. It then turned in my direction and began running. I slowly shifted the weight off my legs and cautiously crawled behind the log I was sitting on and laid prone. I was wearing all black, so I had good faith that he would not see me. My vision was obstructed by the log in front of me, and as a cloud passed in front of the gibbous moon, it grew darker.

For what must have been less than a minute, although it felt much longer, I did not hear anything except the eerie howling of winds and the gentle brushing of snow against the road. Then I heard a sound that I did not at first recognize as footsteps on the road. They were so faint and slow-paced that I thought they might be rhythms of the wind. Though, as I distinguished them to be what they truly were, my heart began to pound for I knew they were the figure's footsteps. I dared not poke my head over the log. The footsteps grew nearer and nearer. And nearer. Then just about when I thought he would approach the log I hid behind, I heard him turn on his heels and begin lurching away.

I cautiously raised my head then shifted into a crouching position. I saw that the figure, who was now bounding like a wolf after prey, was headed in the direction of my house. This terrified me wholly for there was really no way to get to my house without either traveling on the road that Christian Hill stemmed off of. Elm Street is the name of it. Going a long roundabout way to me was greatly unfavorable, and since my house was beyond the turn onto Christian from Elm Street, the figure would either stay on Christian, turn in the direction from which I would be coming, or turn towards my house, the direction I would be going. This left me with two options: take Glenview, the road in the direction opposite of which the figure was headed, or follow far behind the figure, in hope he would not turn or hear me. Now I know which may seem like the better answer, but I had already decided somewhere deep down in my brain that I would follow the figure. I would like to say I was going to follow and investigate him, but really I just wanted to get home, and that was the quickest route. Besides, there was always someone about the roads of Upton at night, if not police, plenty of groups of teenagers walked about at night, skateboarding and causing mischief. Surely they would be interested in a ghost hunt, or at least my protection.

I walked out onto the road and began heading in the direction the figure had headed. I assume my readers, if any, would know of

24

Upton, and if not can look the road up on Google maps. Why I bring this up, is for a point of reference. After I had been walking for five to ten minutes, I reached the first intersection of Pearl and Christian. I had just been thinking that the figure was probably already at the end of the road, for he had been previously running, when I heard the cacophonous shrill of a girl. At first my rational mind tried to tell me it was a fisher cat; though the scream ended abruptly. Then, to my horror, I spotted the figure yet again. It was manipulating some object in a field in front of a barn that belonged to the first house on the left on Pearl Street. Again I was bitterly terrified at how tall and skinny it was, it looked almost not human. It was standing there at the sharp corner of Pearl and Christian. I felt the most fear I had in my life, for when I noticed what the figure was doing. I realized its purpose in the field with the RV for it was fighting with a dog in the field in what seemed like maybe a rough game of tug, though I could hear the far-off whimpers of the dog, which sounded undoubtedly helpless.

Then the scream again. The figure momentarily looked up with his foot on the dog's chest and then seemed as if he was laughing as he looked up at the moon, then it all at once thrust a knife into the dog's chest. I began running down the hill away from the figure. I thanked the God I did not even believe in, for the figure did not hear me. I could not believe in any God after witnessing that. I told myself I would go and check tomorrow if the thing had attacked the beautiful horses that belonged to the nearby farm, but, come the next day, I could not find the courage to do anything more than take photographs from the safety of my car. Since that day I photographed the places where I spotted the creature. I have not returned to that road or the town of Upton again.

Submitted by An Anonymous Former Upton Citizen, Upton, Massachusetts

. . . .

8.
The Darkest Times

Whittier, California

My husband and I used to live in the apartments between Newlin and Philadelphia Streets. As newlyweds we were as happy as can be to have a place of our own. When we took a tour of the apartment, I was ecstatic! From apartment hunting, I knew this was our home for years to come! A couple of months passed, and we had put finishing touches in our home, but it really never felt like ours. I started noticing I disliked keeping the restroom door closed when I would shower. I would always feel like if someone was there, I would feel so afraid with the door closed. I would only close it when I had people over, and I would feel so scared. Little by little I would see my husband's attitude change. He seemed more moody, more aggressive, and snappy. He was really unpleasant to be around. All our conversations would end in fights. It was really rare to have a heart to heart talk anymore. Our food that was laid out started to spoil within hours. Mind you, bread, potatoes, peanut butter, fruit etc.

I was home alone for quite a bit. My husband worked 10/15/24 hour shifts, so I would be on my own a lot of the times. I would notice the lights flicker when our light bulbs were brand new. Stuff would go missing. Things would not be in the spots that we would leave them in. We would fight with each other because things of mine were misplaced. Things of his were misplaced, and we would just point fingers at each other. The room became heavier and heavier. Not only that, the whole complex started acting weird. It was a four-apartment complex with a house in the front. One night my husband was at work, and I was sick. I had a really bad cold and a mild fever. I rarely get sick. It was about 7:00 pm I went to bed. I took my medicine and knocked out. I left my phone charging a few feet away from our bed. I, always before going to bed, would leave the hallway light on and close the bedroom door.

I had a really bad nightmare. A demon disguised as my husband wanted me to let him in the house. In my gut I knew it was not him. I told him "no, I wouldn't let you in. " He kept insisting, growing irritated to let him in my home, and I kept saying no. I said he was not my husband and that I demand he leave my husband and go away. I could feel it breathing in my face, and it started to laugh. This evil laughed and said "it's too late. " He said that he owned my husband and that my husband was not as strong as he has made himself seem. I kept screaming at it to leave us alone. I remember thinking to myself I needed to call my husband. I looked at my phone as if I was awake. I felt like it was a dream within a dream. As I tried to reach for my phone, the demon disguised as my husband told me that there was nothing I could do to help myself. I started praying and asking my guardian angels and God to protect us and protect our marriage. I kept praying keeping that thing as far away from me as possible until I awoke. I was drenched in sweat. My clothes, my bed, my hair, and my sheets drenched in sweat!

I jumped off the bed, and the door to my room was open! The light in the hallway was flickering, so much so it just turned off. I turned on all the lights in the house, the living room, the kitchen, the bathroom, the front door light, which never, ever turned on after my dream. I was in the room. I texted my husband what happened when the lights in my room start to flicker. There was no way, all the lights in the house would go off and start to flicker when we changed all of them to new ones when we moved in! I was changing my clothes as quickly as I could, and I called my husband. As soon as I called him the fan above our bed went on. I got my keys. I got my phone, and I bolted out of our apartment. My husband got off his shift at 10:00 pm, and it was 9:00 pm. With no family nearby I waited in my car until he got home which was like around 11:00 pm. I was crying. I was scared, and I did not remember if I locked our doors.

When he arrived we both went upstairs. Our front door lights were off. He walked in the house; everything was normal. I explained to him what happened. We went to our room, and the light in the hallway was turned back on. I prayed until I fell asleep. I had to wake up the next morning to go to work. Things after that night had never been the same. People surrounding the neighborhood were acting even stranger, and I could not take it anymore. We found a loophole in our lease, and we left our apartment one month before our lease ended. We loved our landlords, but we hated our home. It tore us apart; the demon in that home wanted to tear us apart. It found its strength through our fights and our fear.

Since moving we rarely fight. We are closer than ever. When we talk about our first home, it ends up into a conversation of bad times and bad spirits. Apartment D is a haunted apartment. They provoke, and then they attack. When you start to see that your food is moldy and your plants start to die when you buy your food fresh and you take care of your plants, know that you have a very bad spirit or a demon. It will go for the weakest person. Be aware and remember your faith can protect you, even in the darkest times.

Submitted by Zoe, Whittier, California

. . . .

9.

My Vision

In 1990 I worked on the restoration of the Citadel in Brenham. On the second floor another guy and I were sanding doors. We would take them down, put them on saw horses, and sand with a pad sander. I saw out of the corner of my eye a woman walk by. This other person and I were the only people on site at the time. The woman walked up to a window wearing only a man's large white dress shirt. She had black hair a little longer than shoulder length a little wavy but not curly. The hair could have been a dark brown almost black in color. She was white skinned, very light complexion with sad eyes. Her eyes maybe brown. She was probably in her high twenties to mid-thirties. If she was older she took great care of herself when she was alive. She was slim and maybe five foot eight or so. I think she had a ring on her finger, but if so it was on the wrong finger. The way she walked by I would have only seen her right hand. A single diamond seems right on a silver ring. Her nails were clear, not painted, and not too long. I think she wore a thin silver chain around her neck with a matching diamond. She walked gracefully but determined. She made eye contact with me on the way to the window as if she wanted me to see her. She was barefoot, and the man's dress shirt went to her mid thighs fitting very loose on her. It was long sleeved and closed or buttoned up, but the neck was open.

I must have taken my hand off of the sander in watching her, so I had let my machine stop. The other guy stopped his sander, so I glanced at him. Then I heard the window slam shut one of the windows in the back of the house. I looked back at the window, and she was gone. The guy that I worked with ask if I saw her. I told him that I did, and I ask if he had he said no. He turned his sander back on and went back to work. I did the same. I asked him about it at lunch, he said that another guy that used to work there saw her. He had told him about her then he quit. The same

29

week on the third floor I was standing in front of the middle window looking down on what would be the far right side of the house, if you were looking at it from the front or highway side. I was there alone looking down at what used to be a shed. I do not know if it is still there or if it was only temporary. We kept tools in there. I was thinking about trying to hide in the shed to smoke. The owner did not allow smoking on his property, and he was known for watching from a distance. I felt as if someone pushed me on both shoulders hard. I had a falling feeling. It seemed that there was only one window there, and it was a lot larger than the little one that I was looking out of. What I saw hit the ground looked like a woman in a white dress. It was like a vision.

The other stuff was still there, but like I could somehow see a changed landscape. I feel like she was telling me that she was pushed to her death, and it was covered up as if it was a fall. I never saw her again and even tried to talk to her when I was there alone. I woke up from a dream thinking about it today, so I grabbed my phone to try to look up accidental deaths or someone falling from that window. I found this web site (www. ghostsofamerica. com) so I posted the story, if any one knows more about who she is or was, let me know. I did speak to the carpenter who built the stairs in the grand room and told him the story. He said that before I started working there he had replaced on the third floor on each end the large windows with three smaller ones that I do not think even open. However, the large ones did open and were big enough that someone could have been pushed from one. He knew that I had no knowledge of the reconstruction. This woman was murdered there. I am sure of it, but I cannot find anything that even acknowledges what happened there, nor have I heard any stories. I was born in Brenham and grew up there. I left at the age of nineteen. I have only been back to visit family a few times.

Submitted by John, Brenham, Texas

. . . .

10.
Evil Stepdad

Littlefield, Texas

This is about the train tracks in Littlefield, Texas. My family and I lived there when I was 8. Every morning my step dad would take us to school and on his way he would pick up his coffee.. But this morning he decided that while we got dressed he would run and get coffee.

He left, we waited and waited. He never came back and my mom got to worrying. I didn't, I couldn't stand my step dad. He was mean. Then we got a call from the hospital saying that he had been in an accident with a train.

They said that he was listening to music and didn't hear the train coming. But I don't see how because that train would blow its horn so loud and it wouldn't just do it once, no two to three times.

Every morning we would have to wait for that train to pass and it would be louder than his music. I would always get chills and goose bumps on those train tracks. But on this day he went by him self.

The train knocked him out the passenger side of the car.. The back of the car was no more, just the front was intact. They told my mom that if we were with him we would have been dead. I wonder if it was the children that died there Feb 7, 1973..

Did they know that he was mean to children? And they were giving him that same fate that they had. I prayed that he didn't make it but he walked home from the hospital hurt and all.. They didn't release him, he just left on his own..

The reason I tell this story is my step dad attracted ghost to him. Everywhere we lived there were ghosts. We had a car he bought from the bank, it was a one time owner. And the man that owned it took very good care of it..

It was a Pontiac but it was clean, it was a pretty color of green with a white top. The inside was white. The first time he got the car we went out of town to visit his mother. It was dark when we were heading back.

Me and my sister and two brothers were in the backseat, we were all falling asleep. My little brother was just two years old at the time. He just went to screaming and he was like he was stuck to the seat and couldn't move, the rest of us jumped in the front seat with mom.

When we pulled over and turned on the light he was screaming so hard and shaking, when he calmed down he told my mom that a man was holding him and wouldn't let him go. My mom was saying that it could have been her deceased father because at the time she was pregnant with my little sister.

Then about two days later my oldest brother was told to go to the car and get something and it was dark. He returned, he was really white and shaking but he didn't say what had happened. And he didn't have what he was sent for.

My brother didn't like to tell scary stuff around me and my sisters and mom. So he waited and told my step dad, he told him that he went to the car and that the light was on inside. And that there was a man sitting in the front seat smiling at him, he had gray hair and had on a white shirt and tie.

Later my stepdad waited for it to get dark and he decided to tell us about it. And when I tell you that my step dad was evil I mean it. After he told the story I remember feeling scared to death.

So I told him that I didn't want to ever go out to the car in the dark. And that's when he made me go.. I didn't see anything, that was the good thing. He returned the car back to the wife of the man that owned it.

Submitted by Sharon, Littlefield, Texas

. . . .

11.
Pioneer Family

Milliken, Colorado

I grew up on S. Ethel Avenue. I remember many sightings in that home. The first and scariest happened when I was home alone. I swore I heard footsteps on the main level as I was cleaning in my basement bedroom. I went to my door to go investigate, and the doorknob would not turn. There was no lock. I waited a while, and when the footsteps went away I tried my door again, and it opened without a hitch. Scared, I checked all the basement then went up the stairs. I checked the main floor one room at a time until I came to the front door and noticed that it was open, only the screen was closed. I remember vividly closing the front door when my dad and brother left because I would be alone.

I also remember being sure our dog was inside with me. As I looked out the screen door, however, the dog was standing at the open front gate (also something that was closed.) He was barking as if there were a stranger on the other side of the fence line. I looked and saw no one up or down the road, so I called the dog back inside with me. A neighbor called a few moments later to ask if she could borrow some baking powder. She could hear the fear in my voice, so she came over with the intention of debunking my story and setting my mind at ease. I walked her through it all, and then she suggested we explore outside the fence where the dog saw something too. Happy to get out of the house I agreed.

There was a sidewalk outside the fence and a flower bed with a large tree between the sidewalk and the road. Under the tree we found physical evidence of the ghost. An old glass pill bottle from the Milliken Pharmacy at the turn of the century! I saw this grown woman turn sheet white, and we went to her house until my dad returned home. I kept that bottle for many years.

Another time, shortly after my baby sister was born I heard crying. I was home babysitting, so naturally I went to check on her, and she was sound asleep in her bassinet. I kept hearing the crying and wandered through the house. There in the window above the staircase I saw her. She was dressed as you would imagine a pioneer woman, and she seemed exhausted. She was sitting in a rocking chair and trying to hush the baby she held to her chest. She looked up at me, and I just smiled. You know the smile you give someone when you know how they feel and wish you could help, a kind of awkward yet encouraging smile. She kissed the baby's head, and then the crying stopped, and they were gone.

Shortly after my father passed in that house we happened to meet a couple of old ladies. One of them told us how her ancestors had homesteaded right where we lived. She said they got a great deal on the land because no one else wanted it. You see a pioneer wagon had stopped there because they had all come down with illness and did not have the strength to continue on their way. They all passed away and were buried right there on that land. I do not remember how many children, but she did say there was a baby. We had never met her before and had never told her my experiences. I never got her name or saw her again, but I pray that pioneer family may someday find their peace.

Submitted by Rebecca, Milliken, Colorado

. . . .

12.

A Protective Spirit

Long Beach, California

Even prior to moving into the old duplex on Gale Avenue I felt a presence. While outside observing the garage door that needed repair, I felt a bit overwhelmed at the list of things I was mentally making notes of which I wanted to take care of before actually moving in. Just as I was thinking about this, I felt a hand on my shoulder as if someone was reassuring me not to worry and that everything would be all right. I quickly turned around, but no one was there. I then left with a strange feeling about the incident, but I soon enough convinced myself that perhaps I was just imagining the entire situation.

A few weeks later my family and I moved in. It was not long before my sons were telling me that a ghost of a man lived with us, and he was seen more than once in their bedroom. In addition, he had a name and was deemed by the boys as a "good" spirit. I told them to let me know when they see him, which they did. Try as I may, I never saw anything. It left me wondering. I worked at a nearby school and knew the children who lived in the duplex before we did. One day the youngest child who was probably right at the time approached me and said "Ms. Debbie, you know a ghost lives there?" I was shocked. I replied that "no, I didn't know that. " She then went on to explain that there was a ghost in the house, and it was a man. I did not say anything as the bell rang for class, and she ran off. I will never forget that day. I knew she was right. My boys knew, and I recalled the incident I had before moving in.

Months went by, and we eventually had a house guest for awhile. This woman had only been staying with us a few days and announced that something evil was in the house. Hmmm. I did not get that vibe, but nevertheless I explained what she may have seen. She then became defensive and continued to state that this

35

presence was evil. Over time, I saw that she herself had an agenda, and eventually she moved out. However, before she left there was an earthquake one night which left me screaming. I instructed the boys to get in the doorway, cover their heads, and stay there. All of a sudden, he was there! I saw him. She did too. A shadow of a figure appeared in the hallway right in front of my bedroom door gesturing as if to say "don't worry, it'll be all right. " I instantly felt calm; at the same time he was moving down the hall towards the boys' room and vanished. I asked the boys if they saw him just then. They did not. We lived there for five years before relocating to a different area. I feel that he was indeed a protective spirit, and I believe he may still be there as he was with us and with the previous tenants before us.

Submitted by MsDebbie, Long Beach, California
. . . .

13.
The Sound Of Cheering
Gettysburg, Pennsylvania

We were two families in Gettysburg, tenting at Artillery Ridge Campground. That weekend we toured the battlefield extensively, attended a giant reenactment, and rode on horseback over the field of Pickett's Charge. That Sunday marked the end of the re-enactor events. The roads out of Gettysburg were jammed with cars, campers, horse trailers, and even a heavy-duty flatbed truck-trailer rig with four "Napoleon" cannons chained to the top. By 8 o'clock the town was deserted. Our two families, tenting under a large shade tree were virtually the only guests still at the campground. We hit the sleeping bags early. I dozed off at around 10 pm. It was around midnight when I awoke to the sound of a great multitude cheering. It sounded as if a sports stadium was located right nearby, with a full crowd cheering constantly. There was the sound of a drum roll too, no rhythm, just drums rolling endlessly.

It was about midnight. Surely there would not be a reenactment in the early morning hours. It dawned on me what I was hearing when my friend in the next tent asked "are they holding a re-enactment in the middle of the night?" I replied, "No, I think that's the 1863 battle. " Both families came out of their tents. My friend's two kids and his wife were standing and listening. So was my wife. The sound was superbly clear. And it was, without any doubt, the sound of human voices, and a long drum roll. Some of the party thought they heard the snapping and popping of musketry, a sound we had come to know very well that weekend. I did not hear the muskets, but I heard the neighing and screaming of horses.

So as we stood around under a crystal clear starry sky, the sounds went on and on. Fatigue won out over fascination. While the sounds of the battle still raged, I went back to the tent and fell right asleep. An hour later I awoke with a start. The cheering was continuing, but I had had enough and went back to sleep and slept until dawn. During the cheering I made a tour of the park but did not find a public address system or speakers of any kind. No one else was there to make the noise. Across the street was Cemetery Ridge. There were no nearby stadiums or arenas. The park was closed and empty -- at least of the living.

This was actually the second time I had heard the drums and the cheering. I had camped at Artillery Ridge years before and woke up to the sounds of cheering and a long drum roll. My wife and daughter did not wake up, and I assumed that I was hearing some kind of July 4 weekend sports event. The second time I had no doubts but plenty of witnesses. I wonder if anyone else has encountered this ghostly sound of battle.

Submitted by Brian, Gettysburg, Pennsylvania

. . . .

14.
Childhood Memories

Merced, California

I will do my best to remember these series of events in order as it was so long ago. I grew up in the rural neighborhood of East Merced. The street was called Stretch Road. I could see and hear the sounds of the Santa Fe trains daily. I remember as a kid after a huge storm in the early 1980s that blew our backyard fence completely down and exposed what seemed to be a good two-acre of overgrown land. What was fun was those large lots of homes completely surrounded this land. Anyhow I started having visions of seeing large oversized bugs in our front room that simply made no sense. It frightened me, but I simply chopped it up to my imagination. Here is where things started to get eerie.

We used to have a very large laundry/storage building that had two entrances both facing the east side of the building. This building would scare the hell out of me every time. I would have to go with either mom or dad in order to enter. It was beyond creepy. Sometimes I would have to take a laundry basket there for my mom, and I dreaded each time. Mind you, I never said a word about what I had already witnessed and was feeling. As a child my room was at the far west corner of the house that was practically a few yards to this other building. At night, like late at night, many times as I lay on my bunk bed I would stare out to the kitchen because we always had the light on over the sink. This mass would begin to form in the top right corner of my room opposite of the door and slowly begin to envelop the room moving towards me. I WAS the object it was targeting and inside I knew it. I would simply lie there in utter fear staring into it hoping it would not touch me. Before too long it would get so close I could feel its energy, and I would slide down off my bed and run into the shared bathroom. I would be petrified!

I remember one night I was trying to sleep through the night only to be pushed from off the top bunk onto my toys below on the ground. Other nights I would look into the kitchen, and in the ambient light I could see what looked like soldiers in a march with large hats and muskets. I never got an eerie feeling seeing that. I was more intrigued. Anyway this went on for many years. Now I am much older and having many more experiences as I have gotten older and living in Grass Valley. I have since then expressed extreme interest in the paranormal as I find it interesting, motivating, and in many respects a personal journey to answer questions from my past.

Submitted by D in Sacramento, Merced, California

. . . .

15.

Have You Seen Her?

Clinton, Tennessee

In the early spring of 1990, I was briefly staying with a relative who lived off Foust Carney Road. One night I was driving on Clinton Hwy towards Clinton after seeing friends in the Broadacres neighborhood in Powell. At midnight exactly, I was stopped at the light at the intersection of Clinton Hwy and Edgemoor Road. A guy on his tractor at the intersection to my right passed through his green light onto Edgemoor Road. I remember thinking it was a weird time of night to be on your tractor, but... Whatever. When my light turned green I passed through the intersection, and as I did it felt like every hair on my head stood up straight. It was very strong and weird sensation. The sensation continued as I was driving in the left lane up the road.

I had my bright headlights on, and nothing else on the road, when I saw in passing, in the right lane beside me a very young girl crossing, possibly ten to twelve years old, walking on the right side of the road. She was barefoot and in a straight little colorless dress with spaghetti straps. Not enough attire for a cool early spring night. She also had her head turned away from me, at an acute angle looking way over her left shoulder. She never even glanced at my car, or looked where she was going, even though I passed pretty close to her. The powerful hair raised effect was still with me, and even though, being female, I have stopped to help other females on the road at night at different occasions. I could not have stopped for her for any reason whatsoever. I should probably mention that I was well past the Zion Cemetery, and closer to Foust Carney Road, where I was turning off, when I saw her.

I was scolding myself for not stopping the rest of the way to the house, and was feeling guilty and still weirded out by the time I arrived. I went ahead and called the Sheriff's office about the young girl being on the road like that, and where I had seen her, and they said "yes, we know about it already. " The woman I spoke with sounded kind of irritated, and then she said "everybody who's called about her says she's in a different place. " I hung up the phone feeling kind of bemused and foolish, when it consciously hit me. As I had been driving up the road, with my brights on she would have been crossing right in front of me. My headlights had never picked her up! So years now after the fact, still not sure what I saw. Anybody else ever seen her?

Submitted by Anonymous, Clinton, Tennessee

. . . .

16.
She Was Reading My Book
Roswell, New Mexico

In 1966 my husband and I lived on Shartell Avenue. I was expecting our first child. He went to Job Corps in a school on 5th Street (walking distance). One morning he got up, got ready, and left the apartment. I remember him kissing me then I went back to sleep. Now he always made sure the door was locked when he left. I woke up to a bone crushing cold, and I thought someone had come in the apartment through the bedroom door that led outside. No one was there. I was still half asleep, so I turned on my side to go back to sleep chalking it up to crazy early morning nonsense.

When I turned over and looked from my bed out to the living room much to my surprise there was a young woman rocking in my rocking chair reading my book! My mind said "you are not seeing this. Go back to sleep," and I did. I also did not have my glasses on, but I could see some without them. This is where it gets weirder. When I got up later I looked at my book, and the page was not where I left it. I asked my husband when he came in for lunch if he had messed with my book, and he said no. I went to my landlady and asked what had happened to the people in our apartment. The tale she told me was interesting in light of what I had just seen. It seemed that the couple and their baby were coming down Comanche Hill and had a head on collision killing the woman and the baby which were buried together. I did not see the baby in my vision, but I did see the woman. This happened when I was fifteen or sixteen, and I am now sixty-five years old. To me it is like it happened yesterday. I have never and will never forget this.

Submitted by Glitz, Roswell, New Mexico
. . . .

17.
Pogonip

Santa Cruz, California

Five of my friends and I were walking through Pogonip, the forest behind Merrill College at UCSC, late at night along the railroad tracks. We had been walking back to campus from The Garden of Eden when we saw an extremely bright light behind us on the railroad tracks. It made a sound like a train, so we all got off of the tracks and waited for it to pass. The light came closer and closer, but it never passed us. The light just went out, and its sounds evaporated. We never saw a train or anything else pass.

We told the story to some other kids from UCSC, and two other guys had a similar story to ours. They were cross country runners and were running on the tracks early in the morning. It was very foggy when a train passed them, but they said that the people on it were all looking at them with blank faces. They ran further without thinking much about it when they saw a man in the middle of the tracks hacking at a tree that had fallen over the tracks with an axe. They did not understand how the train had crossed the tree, or how the man had found the tree so quickly if it had just fallen. They kept running when another train passed them going the opposite direction. They decided to run back to the man to see if the train had hit the tree, but when they got to the spot that he was hacking at before he was not there, and neither was the tree! It creeped them out so much that they ran directly back to campus.

Submitted by Jazmin, Santa Cruz, California
. . . .

18.

Mr. Ghost

Longwood, Florida

I live in the Sweetwater Springs subdivision located on the west side of Longwood, FL next to the Wekiva River and Wekiva State Park. My home was completed in early 1989 as a spec home. It sat vacant for a while and then became a rental for a year. We bought the house in mid-1990. Soon after moving in I occasionally began to see a fast moving shadow. I have healthy skepticism, so I did not say anything about it at first. For one thing, the shadows moved very fast. So it was hard to be sure exactly what I saw. Secondly, the shadows were translucent. I could see through the human form that "grayed out" what was in the back of it. However, I could not see much detail.

Over the last twenty-four years we have gotten to know our "Mr. Ghost," as we call him, quite well. He has become far more adept at communicating, and my wife and I have become more capable of sensing him when he is around. He does come about half the time when we call him although if there are people visiting that he does not know, he keeps his presence (assuming he is there) clandestine. The beginning of significant events began when I saw a large, bright-white "ball of light" that hovered in mid air right in my path, not more than ten feet away. When I saw it, I heard (not with my ears but with some other pathway) a voice say "It's fine that you know I'm here, but it's best we don't communicate. " It was a firm and fatherly (but, not stern) voice (almost instructional.) As soon as it had delivered the mail, it whooshed away. That was about sixteen years ago.

Since then Mr. Ghost has learned to make white noise over the intercom when he is upset if a family member has been away for a long time. He would turn lights back on that I have turned off. He has cut down a set of venetian blinds (these were easily ten feet across) held by six nylon cords. The cords were cut so cleanly. I do not think I could have done as well with a scalpel. He can turn on, or turn off, the cable box and surround sound amplifier. For some reason he does not bother to turn on the actual TV. Maybe as long as the cable is on, he does not need the actual TV? I have no idea. Usually he is most active (he often wakes me up, I think for nothing more than to have some company) at 3:00 am to 3:30 am. He has moved a pen, three times in a row (within about a minute) off of a level counter top. The pen had a pocket clip on it, so it could not roll at all.

One night (this was just about two weeks ago) I was in bed watching TV with my wife sleeping next to me. All the lights were off, and the only light in the room was from the TV. I sensed Mr. Ghost was standing at the door of the bedroom, and I waved to him and went back to watching TV. A minute or so later he got my attention again, and I waved to him again and said "you can come in. " For whatever reason, he rarely comes into our bedroom and prefers to stay at the west end of our house. I went back to watching TV, and about ten seconds later, wham! It felt like a St. Bernard had hit the side of the bed at a full gallop. The king-sized bed really shook, and you could hear the impact over the TV. I guess I am used to him because I just laughed. Obviously I was not paying the attention to him that he was looking for.

There are so many instances, and so many different things he has done over twenty-four years. We are not scared of him, but we do take notice when he reaches out because usually it means he is upset about something. At first we had no idea. But now, we think that whenever one of us is away for a long time, especially if it is my autistic son, he gets very concerned. When my older children were in high school, if they came home late, as soon as they walked in the door, they used to feel what they described as "spider webs" all over their face and neck. No matter how they rubbed, the feeling would not go away. I do not know whether he was admonishing them or hugging them. I suspect it was the former.

46

I have had lots of cats and two dogs. They have not seemed to have reacted to him at all. Either they are used to him or they do not sense him. I cannot tell you for sure which it is.

Well, there is a lot more to tell, but this is too long already. We feel as though he is a part of our family, and frankly if he left, we would be saddened.

Submitted by DCG, Longwood, Florida

. . . .

19.

Cursed Gift

Thomasville, Georgia

I live in a small trailer park in the county in Thomasville. I have heard what sounds like a TV or radio playing inside my house, but I do not even have a TV, and the only radio is beside my bed. My neighbor has experienced the same in her house. Sometimes it feels like my bed is shaking. Sometimes more violently than others, and sometimes it feels like there is something big moving around beneath my bed pushing and sliding around on the underside of my mattress. The same neighbor said they have felt an uneasy feeling in one of their bathrooms, and it feels like something is shaking the toilet from time to time. There have been times during the night and early hours of the morning, I have seen what looks like a person moving very quickly.

Three days ago I left my house to walk to the neighbors, and they were with me. At the end of my house it looked like someone was standing in the window. I only caught a glimpse and turned to run as I thought someone was in my home. My daughter was with me and saw this also, except she gave a more detailed description of what she saw. She said it was a girl in a white dress with blue eyes and long curly blond hair. I immediately told her to wait outside while I checked the house. I took my dog inside with me. I checked everywhere that someone could be or hide. There was nobody there. When I went to the room that I saw someone in the window of, there was only one thing amiss. There was a wooden cross that had been hanging on the wall at the head of the bed, and I found it off the wall. It was lying at the end of the bed. I know it was hanging sturdy, and there was no way it could have just fallen down.

Neighbor also said she knew that at some point in time someone committed suicide in her home. I have been trying to search through property records, but it is hard when it is a mobile home,

48

and addresses have changed through the years. I do not know what we saw, or what the noises we are hearing are all about. I hope I do not ever see anything like that again! It scared me so much I ran and tripped over a wheel barrel handle in my neighbor's back yard, sending me flying for a loop. I had pretty bad bruise on my leg, hit my head, and injured my back. Regretfully, this probably will not be the only post I make.

This "problem" seems to have been with me for as long as I can remember. Things got so bad in one of my homes; I called in Paranormal Investigators. I was not happy with the end result. Their psychic medium told me I am a psychic medium, and so are my children. That it runs in bloodlines. My mother and my grandmother were the same way, but they were able to suppress it. I am not. I was basically told your house is not haunted; you are. He explained that many people with those kinds of abilities in one house makes it a lighthouse for spirits, good and bad. They know who can see and hear them and will come to you if you can see/hear them. Some call it a gift; I say it is the gift that is a curse. I do not want to hear and see these things!

Submitted by D, Thomasville, Georgia

. . . .

20.

She Is Following Me

Twin Falls, Idaho

In Twin Falls ever since I was sixteen I have had something following me, I think. At the childhood home on Grandview I consistently felt something walking on my bed at night as well as one time of three extremely loud bangs on my front door. I moved away to Arizona and had no problems. When I moved back to the same house the activity started again. I moved to a house by the courthouse and saw a girl as a reflection in a TV that was off standing right next to me the very first night I moved in. My son (who was three at the time) started behaving strangely and finally told me a man named "James" was telling him to act this way or he would hurt me. He said he saw this man every night in his room. This went on for at least a year.

Then for the next four years I saw a dark shadow every night in the room between the kitchen and living room. I heard child's laughter and a feeling of intense panic every time I saw it. My son said he would see it all the time too. I moved out of that house after five years, but when my son would visit his dad there he said he would still see it sometimes. However, at the house I moved into my husband, I, and my son would see a girl and hear laughter, knocking, and voices. Then we moved again to a fairly new house, and nothing happened for a while. Then I saw a girl child AGAIN one night. It was a full apparition standing in the office, and I thought it was my four-year-old daughter, so I asked "what are you doing?" It then took off and ran up the stairs giggling. I could hear the footsteps running the whole way, so I got up and followed it up the stairs. My daughter was sound asleep in her bed.

My son that was seeing things before also told me he woke up one night to a girl standing over him pointing and laughing. I constantly heard movement in this room upstairs and coming down the stairs even when my children were not home. In our basement (completely finished) it was so dark even with the light coming through the windows, and it was very cold. The air in there was very thick, and we always had a feeling of not being alone.

Submitted by Steph, Twin Falls, Idaho

. . . .

21.
Kachina Dolls

San Jose, California

In the 1980s I started collecting "Old Western" items including Hopi Kachina dolls. I purchased an intricately made sacred Kachina doll from a man who warned me that Kachinas act as lightning rods for Native American spirits, but I thought this was an urban legend. I put the Kachina on display in my living room. About two weeks later I hosted a dinner for four of my girlfriends who were in a 7:30 am company-sponsored golf tournament. I put them in the bedrooms while I bedded down on the couch. I did not sleep well and got up around 3:00 am to get a glass of water and go to the bathroom.

As soon as I lay back down on the couch I heard a man's voice chanting in the hall and looked up to see a ghostly man coming straight towards me. He was about six feel tall and very thin. He was dressed in Native American clothing. He was shaking a rattle in his left hand and doing a Native American dance while he chanted. He was swirly white and completely opaque. I was terrified! I did not know what to do, so I jumped up and made the sign of the cross over him. He slowly dissipated and was gone in three or four seconds.

I was so shaken that I sat up with the lights on the rest of the night. I did not tell anybody as I was afraid they would think I was crazy. After the golf tournament everyone went home, and I went home to relax. I got a coke and went to open the French doors, so I could sit on the deck. I stopped dead in my tracks. Hovering at the edge of the deck was a furiously swirling cloud in the shape of a man. I watched as it moved back and forth then shot straight up and disappeared. I was scared to death.

The next week I took this Kachina and the others in my collection to an art consignment shop. I told the shop manager about the

52

haunting and told him to warn whoever bought it about what I had experienced. I never saw another ghost in my house. This story is true, and I will swear on a stack of Bibles that it really happened. So be careful of what you bring into your house.

Submitted by Dee Dee, San Jose, California

. . . .

22.

Shadow

Valier, Pennsylvania

I have lived in Valier for sixteen years. When my daughter was about three, she had an imaginary friend named "Shadow. " We took it with a grain of salt and pretty much ignored her when she spoke of "Shadow. " It got to the point she was carrying on full conversations and interacting with well "no one. " In 1999 I was building my pool and hand digging the walls. I remember looking up at the swing set as my daughter was as usual carrying on a full conversation with "nothing. " However, what caught my eye was that both swings, hers and the empty one, were swinging simultaneously in time. When I looked back to take a double take the empty swing was fluttering sideways as if a small child had just jumped off it.

A week or so later I was tied up in an engine rebuild, and my daughter was bugging me, so I said to her "why don't you play with Shadow?" This three-year-old told me "Shadow had to leave; she said she had to go to Brooksville, and it would take her a week to get there. " My daughter never heard of Brookville, PA, and it would take a child about a week or so to walk there. Shadow, to the best of my knowledge never returned.

Note: there have been thousands of Indian arrow heads found in this town. Shadow is likely an Indian name. The topography of the town is that it is three-quarters surrounded by water which makes it primo Indian settlement and/or burial ground as they believed spirits could not pass over water.

Submitted by Five ohh, Valier, Pennsylvania

. . . .

23.
Strange Feeling
Prairie Grove, Arkansas

I have always had the ability to see and hear things others could not. When I was twenty my husband and I lived with his parents in a small house on County Road 206. This place was eerie, and I had so many experiences there. I heard footsteps when no one else was home. Rushing out of my room thinking someone had broken in, I found the doors and windows were all locked, and nobody was there. I would wake up at night hearing voices outside our bedroom window not really being able to hear what they were saying. My husband never heard anything. He is a seriously heavy sleeper. I was outside playing with my infant daughter when I saw a man I did not know standing next to the house. When I looked at him he turned and walked behind it. I went to ask him if he needed something, and in the two seconds it took me to run around there he was gone. I searched all around the house, in the house, scanned the woods, (though in two seconds it would have been impossible for him to have gotten into the woods) and checked inside. I would get the feeling of being watched or followed around the house.

A couple of things I did not personally experience happened to my mother-in-law. One day (long before I moved in) she was looking for the deed to the house, and she had searched the house all day long. She could not find it anywhere. She was about to give up when she heard a woman say "it's in the pink bag in the closet. " Knowing there was not a pink bag in her closet, she went to the closet in the other bedroom and dug until she reached the bottom of a pile. There was a small pink purse with the deed folded up inside it. One night after my husband and I moved out she and my father-in-law were lying in bed when they heard people running around outside. My father-in-law went to investigate, but nobody was outside. They went back to bed, but the sound continued. Then they began hearing people shouting "hurry! Hurry up, please. They're burning!" and "get some more buckets! " and a woman screaming. My mother-in-law did some research on the property. She found out that around the time of the Civil War a family lived on the property, and their house was set on fire. Some family members made it out, but the man's wife and two of his children did not. The entire family was buried in a cemetery just up the hill from the house.

On Highway 265 leading out to Hogeye there is an open field next to a garage (it used to be called Boyz Under Tha Hood.) I would always get a feeling of dread and sadness when we drove past it heading to see his parents'. My husband asked me one day why I always shivered when we drove by there, and I told him the truth. I told him "I feel like someone is buried there who is not supposed to be. " He told me I was crazy. Fast forward a couple of months, we were sitting in my in-law's living room, and my mother-in-law who researches and documents cemeteries for the state started talking about a cemetery they found in a field just down the road. My husband looked at me funny, and his mom asked what was wrong. I asked her if it was the field next to the garage, and she said "yes, it was. " She asked how I knew. I told her that I would get that eerie feeling that someone was buried there that should not be. She gasped and her eyes went wide. She proceeded to tell us that it was an old family cemetery, but someone was buried there that did not belong with the family. A man was arrested in Fayetteville for murdering his wife and died in jail awaiting his hearing. They had nowhere else to bury him, so they put him in that cemetery.

My husband while still not completely a believer does not question when I get strange feeling as much anymore. I have so many more experiences in so many more different towns, but I will save them for another day.

Submitted by Tiffani, Prairie Grove, Arkansas

. . . .

24.
Waiting To Be Invited

Barstow, California

In 1992 my three children and I left Arkansas and moved back to my hometown in Barstow, California. We stayed with my mother for about two months and then rented a small two-bedroom house. My niece, who was sixteen, also moved in with us. My children were two, four, and ten at the time. We lived there for about two months when I ran into an old friend and asked him over. That was when things started happening.

My kids were watching TV in the living room, and my niece was in the room we shared, so my friend and I had gone in my boy's room to catch up on the past few years since I had moved. He was lying on the floor and had dozed off. Out of the corner of my eye I saw a shadow and then heard a loud pop in the corner of the room. (We had no animals at the time). Startled, I got up, went into my own room, and left him on the floor sleeping.

Another time I had gone to bed. My niece had a friend of hers visiting with her in the living room. All of a sudden I could not move. It felt as if something was holding me down. I tried to yell, but all I could get out were noises as if I had a gag covering my mouth. My niece heard me and came to the bedroom door. She thought I was dreaming, but she said my eyes were open. I saw her look in, so I know I was not dreaming. She told me afterwards that she tried to come in, but something would not allow her to. After that everybody thought I would high tail it back to Arkansas. I told everybody that no ghost was going to scare me out of the very first place I have had on my own. Going back to my ex was not an option. After that I had my friend move in. Whenever that thing tried to hold me down again, he was right there to scare it off. Although he never actually saw anything, he knew when it was happening.

Another time my niece was in the living room and saw a reflection in the TV of a pair of legs behind her. She immediately turned off the TV and went to bed. A lot of my niece's friends said they felt weird as soon as they walked into the house, so they would usually talk outside. One afternoon I was sitting in my room and said out loud to whatever was in my house to show itself. I turned towards the bedroom door, and on the wall next to it was an image of someone crouched down with their hands in front of them like something was going to hit them.

I lived in this house from August 1992 until February 1993. The only reason I moved from this house is because my friend was getting custody of his two children, and the house was too small for all of us. After we moved all of the weird things stopped happening except for one thing. After we got settled into our new house I spent a lot of time in my garage. Once I found out how much I enjoyed making things with wood. My neighbor would come over and bring her dogs. The dogs would stare up at the corner of my garage for up to thirty minutes at a time without moving. I also had cats that would do that from time to time. My neighbor believed in the paranormal and joked that it was my ghost waiting for me to ask it to come in. I lived in that house for twelve years, and other than the animals staring at the corner, nothing ever happens like in that first house.

Submitted by Terri, Barstow, California

. . . .

25.
Possessed Mother

Youngstown, Ohio

I used to live in Youngstown, Ohio from the age of 8 till I was 17. I was adopted, and we lived in a house on Idora Ave. I debated about telling this story because of the skeptical folk out there, but they said that the truth is the light. So, here it is.

My adopted mother and I moved into this lovely house when I was about 8 or so from Boardman. My mother loved the house as I did also because it was much more spacious than our small little apartment in Boardman. The first day we moved in I was rooting around in the attic, and I found these incredibly old books about witchcraft. I showed them to my mother who immediately threw them out. At first everything was pretty normal there, save for the madness I was enduring from my adopted mom, but that's another story.

Anyway, right around the time my mother made the attic my bed room things started to change. I would have strange dreams and wake up in other parts of the bedroom which was actually 3 rooms in one (the attic was huge.) I was also waking up to feeling something scratching my legs and feet. I was terrified and almost too afraid to tell my mother due to the whipping I was sure to encounter. So I kept it to myself until my mother started showing signs of being affected by this presence. My mom was a drinker and what started to happen when she drank is this. She would seem to take on the characteristics of someone else. Her voice would change; she began walking with a limp and other things that I knew weren't quite right.

I confided in my grandma Kay at the time and really she didn't know what to tell me other than to pray, so I did. Well, one evening I went to bed early and was awakened to a voice telling me to go downstairs and pray for my mother. I was 12 by this

59

time, so I just jumped up and went downstairs and prayed at her bedroom door. NOW (this is where it gets deep.) As I was praying I heard a voice come out of my mother, and it said "help me!" but her lips didn't move! So I ran over to her and laid my hands on her and began to shout and pray as loudly as I could! Then another voice came out of her, and it sounded like an old man, the voice said "LEAVE ME ALONE!" That was NOT my Mother speaking, so I pleaded the blood of Jesus and screamed. I ran out of her room only for her to awaken moments later crying asking me what had happened. Now from that moment on the house was alive with paranormal activity.

I also recall one morning when my mother and I were arguing in the kitchen, in mid-sentence the kitchen table levitated and split right down the middle and broke in half right in front of us both! Also my Mother suffered with this "spiritual attack" for many years; however, I left home at 17 and never looked back. My Mother has since passed away. God rest her soul. And because of what I experienced there it prepared me for the supernatural life I was to have in my near future.

This account I am telling is real, true and absolutely NO fabrication. It doesn't matter to me who believes it or not now because it happened.

Submitted by Kandiss, Youngstown, Ohio

. . . .

26.

The Ghostly Beach Comber
Isle Of Palms, South Carolina

This strange encounter happened on the beach near 21st Avenue. I am curious to know if anyone else has had a similar experience they would like to share. I grew up on the Isle of Palms several blocks north of the Front Beach Pier. Last week I was visiting my folks and decided to walk back from the Windjammer, one of the finest drinking establishments in the Charleston area. So there it is, make of this what you will. It was late (around 1:30 am on February 22nd, 2014) and let us just say I was one satisfied customer.

The beach was deserted with a slight breeze around fifty degrees and mostly clear skies. Passing under the pier I stopped to take a photo of the half-moon shining down on the calm ocean waves. A little ways past the pier I could see the dark shape of someone up ahead strolling toward me. The figure was contrasted by the moonlit white sand and was traveling in my direction about halfway between the shoreline and the sand dunes.

 I was walking close to the water, so it seemed we would be passing at a comfortable distance. Just then I began to feel nauseous, thinking "uh oh... Must have had more to drink than I thought. " Suddenly I felt so bad; I was sure I was going to be sick. I leaned over, but nothing happened. My stomach seemed fine. That was when I noticed a dark figure had stopped right there between me and the dunes about twenty feet away. It was backlit by the distant lights of houses along Palm Boulevard, but I could not make out even an outline of who was standing there.

It was a little unsettling. Hunched over with one hand on my knee, I pointed at it and said "I see you, shadowy figure, standing over there." There was no reply, just a dark presence kind of watching me. Without taking my eyes off it, I resumed walking and was relieved that the shadow also resumed moving in the opposite direction. As my head began to clear it occurred to me how odd the figure was since the light of the moon to my right should have given me a better view of whoever it was. When I looked back the figure was nowhere to be found. There was just an eerie silence. Starting to feel a little spooked, I took the first path off the beach. It began to dawn on me that the strange feeling of sea sickness had vanished as quickly as the Ghostly Beach Comber.

Submitted by Mambo Johnny, Isle Of Palms, South Carolina

. . . .

27.
The Little Girl

Austin, Texas

I was raised by my Grandmother in Central Austin. When I was about 12 we moved far south due to a fire that burned her house down. My Grandmother surprised me with a huge party for my 13th birthday. All of my friends from school and few kids from the neighborhood were invited. We had so many games, candy, cake and drinks. It was so much fun. I did notice a random little girl standing and watching us play from a distance. She seemed sweet but a little odd by the clothes she was wearing. Her clothes were like something kids in the older days would wear. I figured she may have been a neighborhood kid that got invited and I just hadn't met her. I saw her playing on that old swing under our large oak tree. It had been there since we moved in.

The kids decide we'd play hide and seek. So I hid in the barn out back. No one would ever find me there. After a while the kids couldn't find me and I was about to blow my cover when suddenly I heard a small girls voice say (THIS IS MY FAVORITE GAME) I called out who's there ? No one answered but directly behind me the same voice whispered (I KNOW ALL THE HIDING PLACES... I USED TO LIVE HERE.) When I turned around no one was there. I was afraid, so I started walking quickly out from the barn. There it was again. She said (I SEE YOU!) This time the voice was coming from the upper level of the barn. I ran out of the barn scared out of my mind. All the kids were asking what was wrong and where I was but I didn't say a word.

When all the kids we're gone I told my Grandmother. By this time all the kids were grouped up together in line for cake. Everyone except for that little girl. I had a hard time sleeping the next couple of nights. I never played outside anymore. I mostly went to sleepovers or hung out at different friends houses. From time to time I'd look out my bedroom window but never saw her again.

My Grandmother said the little girl was a kind ghost and would never cause us harm. I found comfort in grandma telling me there was nothing to be afraid of. She said the presence of the little girl was a lost soul of a child that wasn't given the attention or life she deserved. I agreed and wished we could give her some closure.

Submitted by Kenny, Austin, Texas

. . . .

28

The Music Conservatory
Saint Mary Of The Woods, Indiana

When I was at a student, I loved to spend time in the music conservatory. It is an ancient building (probably over a hundred years old) with marble staircases, a splendid auditorium, and outstanding architecture. It looks like a scene straight out of phantom of the opera. However, during my four years there, there were some things that were strange.

Music in the basement: If you've been to The Woods, you probably know that there are underground tunnels that are forbidden. However, (being the "rebels" we were) a couple of friends and I decided to sneak into them. There is an entrance near the music conservatory, and it was fairly easy to get into at the time. There were four of us, and we landed in the dark tunnel with nothing but small lights to show us the way. It was not anything too impressive just cobwebbed, concrete tunnels and what not. We had been drinking, so the whole thing was not exactly what I would call scary. Then we heard music.

At first, we did not think anything of it. We knew we were close to the conservatory, so it could be anyone. (Why anyone would go to the conserve to play music past 12:00 am is beyond me) We tried extra hard to be quiet, so we would not get caught. We decided to follow the sound. We kept getting closer and closer, and then it stopped. We stiffened up, because we thought maybe we had been too loud. We stood there for the longest time and finally decided to go back up to the ground level.

When we were above ground again we heard the music again, so we decided to be curious and go into the music conservatory. It was unlocked. As we were walking through there, it was pitch black. We walked quietly, following the sound of a piano. When we had finally thought we nailed the room with the piano, we opened the door. It was pitch black, and the music stopped abruptly. I flicked on a light, and there sat an empty piano.

I had never been so chilled in my life. I KNOW that was where the music was coming from. It felt like someone was in the room with us, but we looked everywhere to find NO ONE. It was quite a sobering fear (having been a little buzzed). We left and never went back to the conserve past dark again.

Submitted by Kelsey, Saint Mary Of The Woods, Indiana
. . . .

29.
The Truth

Williamsburg, Virginia

While visiting Old Williamsburg in November 2013 with my family we took the candle light ghost tour. I witnessed many things, one of which I will share here. At the last stop on the tour at the house where the former occupant curing Colonial times had her carriage reassembled on the back porch I noticed lights. The lights were above and to the left of the roof of the house. They appeared to be lining the drive going up the hill behind the house. It appeared to be white rope lights with a number of yard stick lights. After the tour I asked the guide about the lights on the hill, and she informed me that there were no hills there and went on to tell me that I had a special experience.

My oldest grandson and I both saw and felt many supernatural events during the tour. My seven-year-old grandson's experience was the one that touched me the most. The guide had shared the story with us about the lady attending a ball and became upset. She broke her shoe, so she pulled up her skirt so she could run faster. She then entered the home, ran up the stairs, turned around, and flung herself down the stairs killing herself.

After the tour the guide and I heard my grandson say "stepped on foot. " She asked him if someone had stepped on his foot. He responded "no, the lady. " She asked if someone had stepped on a lady's foot. At this point he got frustrated and with insistence said "the lady stepped on her own foot. " She asked him what he meant and he told her "the lady with the real long dress stepped on her own foot and fell down the steps. She didn't mean to hurt herself, it was an accident. "

At no time during the tour had anyone talked about the appearance of the attire people wore in days gone by. The guide looked at me bewildered and said "now we know the truth. " I feel very blessed with my abilities, but I feel even more blessed by my oldest and youngest grandsons' ability to see hear and feel the supernatural.

Submitted by Anonymous, Williamsburg, Virginia

. . . .

30.
Seeing Is Believing

Louisville, Kentucky

My family moved into an old house in Eastwood, Kentucky when I was thirteen. Just before we moved in, many neighbors told us that there were ghosts in the house and that we would never be able to keep any pets. Supposedly, a very cruel man named Mr. Casey, an overseer of the orchard the house had been built upon, murdered his wife in the attic of our house. It was said that he, also, hated animals and would regularly kill them. (ALL of our pets, indeed, died in very strange, unusual ways.) The first week we moved in, we heard consistent, rhythmic beating of drums every night. (There had been an Indian massacre in the immediate area in the 1790s.) In addition, I would hear a cat meowing underneath my window every night around midnight. My mother and I were so scared, we would sleep together huddled in each other's arms for protection. Doors regularly opened and closed, lights came on and off, strange noises would sound - all on their own. I would often hear whispering and speaking.

One time when I was in the attic, I heard a man speaking so loud, I ran down the stairs as fast as I could, and I would never go back upstairs again. One time, I saw a woman in a white dress outside my window. She kept saying over and over, "Help me. Help me. " I never had a comfortable night in that house, but my father kept saying that what I saw and heard was nonsense. Finally, I went to college, and one time when I visited my parents, my father reported regularly seeing a woman with black hair in his bed or standing behind him as he looked into the bathroom mirror. Then, he too was convinced. Even though I am fairly educated, I never doubt anyone who believes in the paranormal. Seeing is believing.

Submitted by SLA, Louisville, Kentucky
. . . .

31.

Before Moving On

Indian Lake Estates, Florida

Around the summer of 2006 my husband and I moved into a rental house on one of the canals that go out to the lake. My landlord had just purchased this home from a man who was eager to sell his parents' property since it was entrusted in his care while his elderly mom was in a nursing home. The landlord went through and told us what he wanted to keep. Part of our deal was to clean out the house and use or keep whatever we thought was still useful. It was so strange going through someone's belongings, but it gives you idea of who they were. I went through receipts, paystubs, pictures, furniture, and lots of garbage. So I knew the names of the previous owners that lived there.

We had lived there for a few months, and everything was quiet. It was very quiet out there. One day (and I remember it like yesterday) I was alone at home having a day off to do my chores. I went to my bedroom to fold laundry on my bed when I just got this feeling that I was being watched. As I was folding, in my peripheral vision I could see a shadowy figure standing in the hallway. When I looked up no one was there. I continued to ask if someone was there and looked around, but I did not get that feeling or see anything again. This still gives me chills when I recall it. About two days later as I was exiting the gated community I saw on the billboard that there was a memorial service for "Adele" the lady who lived in the house before me. I think she was just checking out the house before she went on to her next home.

Submitted by Jess, Indian Lake Estates, Florida

. . . .

32.
My Grandfather

Gustine, California

My dad inherited his home from his parents on Preston Road in Gustine, CA. One night I fell asleep on our living room couch, and since I was so hard to wake up my mom threw a blanket over me and left me there. Sometime in the early morning I heard the floor in front of the couch screech. I rolled over to see who it was, and it was an older man bending over with his hands on his knees staring at me. He looked like my father, so just for fun I rolled back over waiting for my dad to tap me on the shoulder to get into my own bed. When that did not happen I rolled over to see the man was gone.

My dad was a truck driver, and he would sometimes come home early in the morning, so I got up and looked outside to see if his truck was home, and it was not. I found out later that my grandfather had passed away in our home before I was born. Those days they had the funeral in your home, so I believe it was my grandfather bending down to look at me. He looked just like my dad does now.

Submitted by Rebecca, Gustine, California

. . . .

33.
Things In Our House

My daughter who is four years old has been seeing things since we moved into this house, along with me and my son and my oldest. My husband works about twelve hours a day, and he does not experience it as much. When he does he always has an explanation of some sort for it all. I on the other hand just feel like there is something more to it. Here are some of the things that have occurred.

Our daughter came in one day panicking about a little boy tied to a chair outside behind the shed in which I checked simply because you never know your neighbors. There was nothing. My daughter talked about the little girl who was burned. My daughter would smell smoke, and tell me it was the little girl. The pictures on the walls have been found upside down in the morning flying off the wall, and all the cabinets and drawers in the kitchen would be open at 6 am. We have all tile floors, and you could hear footsteps. Especially on the tile that the grout was coming undone; it would grind when you stepped on it, and you can tell where the footsteps were going. We have heard heavy breathing and muffled voices.

I have actually thought someone broke into my house. We also heard "hey" in a whispering voice. My son who has always slept with no night light and with his door shut out of nowhere started screaming a while back at night. He said there was a yucky head in his room. (He was two years old at the time it started.) He has now been sleeping with his toy shotgun, a night light, and his door open. He also had conversations at 2:00 - 3:00 am. Sometimes he would be screaming bloody murder at those times which he did not do if he slept in his sister's room.

We have always had a feeling of being watched or someone right next to you. When I was in the shower (at 1:00 am) the bathroom door started rattling. I thought someone was trying to get in to use it. No one was awake when I jumped out to open the door. My in-laws have experienced some of it as well such as a picture flying off the wall but not falling. It came out a good two feet. One time my daughter came to me saying "do you hear them mommy?" I asked her "what?" She said "they are saying our names. Can you hear them?" My oldest daughter (seven years old) told me one morning that she woke up because someone tickled her leg. She said when she looked her dad was squatting on the floor. Then he got up and walked out. The thing was that I actually stayed awake all that night until morning (stressed and could not sleep), and my husband never moved out of bed. This one actually really freaked my husband out.

On another occasion I was sitting at my kitchen table with my back to the wall. It was only me and my four-year-old daughter. I had started getting the feeling that something was not right. Then she pointed behind me and said "um um um" I asked "what?" She responded "there is someone behind you mommy. " I said "no, there is not," and she said "no. Look. Mommy, they are all behind you now. Mommy, get up! Mommy! Mommy, they are behind you. Get up!" I started to look behind me because honestly I believed her. At that moment she covered her eyes and screamed. I jumped up and grabbed her up in my arms and ran out of the room. I did not know what was there, but it scared her and me.

Later one day I was lying in one room, and my kids were in another watching a cartoon. I heard footsteps as if someone was wearing tennis shoes. I got up to check. There was nothing, so I went and sat back down. I heard it again. This time I thought it was one of my kids, but they were all still in the room watching the cartoon. I went back trying to shake the feeling and sat down. I heard it again. Knowing my husband was not home, nor could he get in because we have chain locks on all our doors, I got up again to check. Nothing. I started feeling very creeped out but tried to tell myself it was nothing and sat back down. When I heard it again, my broken tile ground, at the point whatever it was would have been by the doorway of the room I was in. As I got up, my oldest daughter screamed. I ran out, and she said she saw a shadow. She pointed right at the spot where the busted tile was.

It has just been a lot of strange things that have happened. I cannot seem to find a way to find out the history of this house, property, or neighborhood, and this is only some of it.

Submitted by Amber, Metairie, Louisiana

. . . .

34.

Sally

Vineland, New Jersey

I grew up in Vineland and lived there until I was eighteen years old when I left for college. You can say I grew up in an okay neighborhood in Vineland. It was minimum on the crime, and it was pretty quiet. However, the house I grew up in had quite a bit of history. It started when I was about fifteen. I lived in this house with my mom, little brother, and little sister since I was seven years old. We never really had any major problems. My sister and I shared a room because she was still very young. It was maybe Christmas, and my aunt bought my sister a porcelain clown. Though it was scary looking my sister loved it. As we were putting up our gifts she laid her clown on the bed, went to the closet, went back, and her clown was gone. We really never found the clown just a foot from it, and that was when we moved.

Later on my mom bought me a glass porcelain doll. I am not a real big doll fan, but I thought it was very pretty. I sat her on my dresser still in the box. However, for some reason the doll head would be turned numerous ways, but the box was never tampered with. One night I was sleeping in the room alone; my sister and brother were at one of the family member's house that night. I woke up to some noise in my bedroom. I was never a really scared person of many things until this night. When I woke up I saw my doll was missing from her box. When I turned around she was on my sister's bed. The following year when I turned sixteen I decided it was time for a change in my room, so I ended up painting it. It was pretty unique, a navy blue with drawn picture frames. This was the time that really made our home haunted.

Odd things in the house started happening. Things that we thought had logical explanations to them. The gas stove was on, and we thought maybe someone did not turn it off. We sometimes got locked out when we knew we had left the door open. One night I slept in our living room on the couch because something kept creeping me out in my room. I was basically hearing a person talking. That night I got up because I heard someone in the living room. When I looked I saw a woman coming down our stairs and going into the kitchen. Then she went through our basement. That was when it started to really scare me. My mom also saw her, and my brother claimed he saw her but would never talk about it. One day we just got fed up and went to the library, and we looked at some old newspapers. We found an article about a fire that happened maybe seventy years or so ago with a picture of our house on fire. It talked about a gas fire. It said the lady forgot to turn off the stove, and she died in the attic looking for her cat to get it out. The attic just so happened to be over my room, but we never saw any steps leading to it.

When we looked at the obituaries of the deaths to see if she was in there, and without a doubt my mom and I picked the same lady. We had never talked to each other about how she looked. Her name was Sally. When we got home that day we went into my room and looked in my closet. There was actually another wall in there. When we opened it it led to steps that went to our attic. We never went up there. We eventually moved out some years later, but we confronted Mrs. Sally and told her we meant her no harm. We never had problems from her again. However, for some reason every time I got a cat it either died or ran away, but my runaway always came back.

Submitted by T.B.N., Vineland, New Jersey
. . . .

35.
Twisted Evil Smile

West Orange, New Jersey

This all happened so fast. My boyfriend and I had a part time job placing directional signs along highways and such. We had a route that started in West Orange and ended in Livingston. I would always drive, and he would get out and place the signs. The town is beautiful and peaceful with lots and lots of trees and amazing homes. It always felt peaceful until I drove up Mt Pleasant Avenue on the West Orange side. I would feel creeped out every time, and my hair would stand on end. I did not know why, and it would be only from where I turned onto Mt Pleasant Avenue until I reached the corner of Merklin and Kelly. I told my boyfriend that I felt sort of scared on this part of the road, and he just laughed it off and told me to stop watching my ghost shows. I just wrote it off as the road being poorly lit and the tree lined street with barely any sidewalks, and it is not really city life like where I live where at 1:00 am there are tons of people and cars around.

One weekend we reached Mt Pleasant Avenue, and I told my boyfriend "this road creeps me out. " As I drove around the bend right after Skyline Drive I saw a girl walking alone in the distance. I pulled over, so he could put up a sign, and I said" this girl is nuts walking on this road with no sidewalk. " At this point the girl was close enough where I could see her a little better. My boyfriend said "who are you talking about?" I said "the girl over there," and I pointed. He asked "what girl?" I thought he was playing around with me since I am into all this ghost stuff even though I get scared, and he really is not. The girl looked like she was in her teens (maybe around seventeen.) She had a pale complexion, and she had long dark hair about midway down her chest. She was wearing a grayish long sleeve shirt with a long skirt to her ankles (I don't remember the color) and some kind of canvas looking sneakers. She had her arms crossed on her chest walking with her head slightly down. I turned to my boyfriend at this point. I was getting annoyed, and I said "stop playing with me she's right there!" The girl stopped walking and was standing there with her head down. My boyfriend said "babe there's no one there. " All my hairs were standing straight up, and I started to shake a little bit because I was thinking "why do I see her and he doesn't?"

My boyfriend got in the car, and the girl started walking again. As I drove past her, I saw her face and it was the creepiest thing I have ever seen. She had a twisted evil looking smile (smirk) on her face. It was like something you would see on paranormal witness, and when I said twisted I meant it literally. The corner of her lip on the right side was curled up and around her eyes were dark circles like Uncle Fester. I said to my boyfriend (who was checking off the list for the sign we just placed) "look! Look! Do you see her now?" He looked up and said "no I don't! You're going nuts!" I was angry because I thought he was still messing with me. I stopped the car and looked back, and the girl was not there. There was no way she could have turned the corner so fast, and if she crossed the street I would have seen her because the left side of the road had more light then the side we were on. I freaked out so bad and my boyfriend was getting freaked out because of how I reacted that I could not drive. That night he drove and placed the signs. I was too scared to get out of the car.

Submitted by Lily, West Orange, New Jersey

. . . .

36.
Uneasy Feeling

Coos Bay, Oregon

I lived in Coos Bay and North Bend all my life. I have lived in haunted places all the time. It was hard for me to avoid them, but only two still haunt me to this day. When I was around seven or eight years old, I lived up Seven Devils in a house that never felt right. I always had stories about what would happen in the house, and so did my cousins and my aunt (who I lived with from six years old to fourteen years old.) We always talked about the lady in black, a little girl, an older man, a bad man, and a man who hanged himself in a tree who we later found out about after my cousin built his tree fort in the same tree.

Anyway from the moment you pulled into the drive way nothing ever felt right about the property or the houses on the property. It always felt like something sinister was watching you. I woke up to an old man staring right at me and a little girl laughing. My cousin had the lights in the bathroom turned off on her, and she saw red eyes. The woman in black woke her up when something was wrong with us kids. When my cousin was sleeping in his tree fort one summer he woke up to a man sitting on a branch. We talked to our landlord, and he told us of a man who hanged himself in the tree. He also told us there was railroads and mines all over the property.

When I went to live back with my dad we moved into a house near Rite Aid and Seven Eleven in North Bend on Virginia and Broadway. When we first moved in I got the same exact feeling I did from the last house I was in. I would hear people talk right outside my bedroom door at night when nobody would be home. I would hear people walking upstairs when I was downstairs, and so did my grandpa numerous times. When I was doing the kitchen my stepmom was lying down with my newborn brother in her room, and out of the corner of my eye I saw a little boy run across the dining room. I did not think anything of it, but then I realized my brother was just born, and it could not have been my little sister because she was with my dad. They were not home!

When I was upstairs getting ready for school (it was my freshman year) I was sitting on the edge of the bathtub, and I turned my head to look for something. Then I saw a pair of muddy work boots. Yes, there were legs attached to the boots. I did not look up because I knew I would not want to know what the thing looked like. It seemed to realize that I caught it standing behind me and walked out of the bathroom. It could not be my grandpa because he was in Washington, and it could not be my dad because he left for work at three in the morning.

When we moved out I was happy, but when we moved up Virginia into the apartments I still had an uneasy feeling of being watched. I never had an experience, but my six-year-old sister swore there was a man in the living room one night. She told my stepmom to listen, and sure enough she heard stuff moving around across the floor. My dad was at work around that time. When my brother came to live with us he had experiences. His room was attached to the living room, and he heard scratches on his wall late at night when everybody was asleep. I now live in Weed, California, and I no longer have any experiences. However, every once in a while I see the occasional shadow at the foot of the bed, and I know it is just my great grandma or my husband's father looking out for us.

Submitted by Breanne, Coos Bay, Oregon

. . . .

37.
More Than We Can See

Louisville, Kentucky

Three years ago I was looking to rent a home. I contacted a friend to see if he had any homes available. He told me he just had a house become vacant the night before. He said the people left in the middle of the night. I did not think much of it. I was just glad he had a home, and the price was great. The next day my children and I went to the address to check it out. It needed a good cleaning, so I worked out a deal to move in without a deposit. The next day my son and I went to start cleaning.

In the back bedroom there was a rug on the floor. We lifted it up and found a weird symbol on the hardwood. I did not think much of it. I just started to clean it off. We were there a few days, and my daughter was in the kitchen playing on the computer, and I heard her scream. She said there was a man peering in the kitchen window. I ran to yell at him, and he was gone. I did not see him, but my daughter was not the type to lie about something like this. As days passed we started to hear scratching in the walls and banging outside towards the back of the house.

One night my daughter was staying the night with friends, and I was home with my son. I was lying on the couch trying to sleep when I started to hear the keyboard on the computer. It was a loud fast typing just like my daughter would type. I rose up and said "Ashley stop being so loud. " Then I remembered my daughter was not home. My son came out of his room that was right next to the living room. As we started down the hall, the noise stopped. We backed up towards the living room. As we got closer to the front door, there were three big bangs on it. I grabbed a bat and opened it. No one was there. It really shook us up.

A few days later I got off from work and picked my children up from their dad's. When we walked in the door I could not believe my eyes. My hallway was full of flies, hundreds of them. There was no garbage in my home. I killed them all and just ignored it. I really did not understand why or how this was going on, and it was winter outside. Later that week my son told me he had been seeing a tall shadow man in his room, and he had taken pictures of him. I started to hear voices in the house whispering, but I never could make out what I heard.

My daughter was staying more with her dad, so I thought I would sleep in the back bedroom. I went to bed and within 10 minutes of lying down I heard a growl in my ear. It was the scariest thing I had ever heard. I jumped up and ran out of that room. I felt like I was being watched. I never slept in that bedroom again. I did not tell my kids about this. I did not want to scare them anymore than they already were. I moved out a few months later. I sometimes ride past that house and wonder what was really in there. I wonder if someone died in there, or the people that rented it before me were practicing some evil religion. I know what me and my children experienced was real, and now I believe in something more than we can see.

Submitted by E M, Louisville, Kentucky

. . . .

38.

A Huge Home

I used to work for a wealthy person who owned a huge home here. He only came there twice a year for two weeks at a time, so most of the time it was shut up. My job was to care take it. It had three levels, and I would vacuum and clean it constantly mostly alone. After a while I started to notice a certain closet door was always open when I came to check on it. I did not think much of it at first, but after a while I noticed it was more often than not. Next was the light being on in the same closet. I began to pay attention to it and made sure each time that the light was off and door closed, but it kept happening. Next, I was vacuuming in a bedroom when the phone started ringing. This house had the ability to call from room to room, and it showed it was calling from the same bedroom to the downstairs. It scared me, and I went outside for ten minutes to calm down. Finally I went back in, and the phone was still ringing. I picked it up, and it showed it dropped the call. I left!

Next time I came back, and I was again vacuuming. I looked over at the phone base, and it was blank. I was thinking "thank god nothing scary. " Right then it showed that someone had picked up the receiver upstairs. Again I freaked out and left. This went on and on. Finally my husband said to lock it to see if anyone else on the ranch was messing with me. I locked it that night, and we had a light snowfall overnight. I woke early and drove over to the house. No tracks in the snow or tire marks. I unlocked the door and started to climb the spiral staircase to the top floor. As I climbed the hair on my neck and arms just stood on end, and I had chills. When I got to the particular bedroom the door was open, and the light was on. When I came downstairs I could hear a buzzing noise. I followed the sound and found the hot tub in the master bedroom was running. It scared me as I had not even been in that room. I just left. I was getting too frightened to be in there anymore! Finally, I went in there one day and just said "I do not know who you are, but you're scaring me, and I'm not here to hurt you. " And it stopped!

I always felt I was being watched in that house too. Even when I was outside, I could feel a heavy brooding presence. I no longer felt that but always felt I was being watched. The house was filled with Native American artifacts and old guns. It was built in a valley where the Utes summered. All this is true, and it happened just like that. I worked with all men, and they just thought I was mistaken, but I knew better.

Submitted by Elizabeth, Walden, Colorado

. . . .

39.
Very Dark Place

Austin, Texas

In the summer of 2012 I was visiting my boyfriend (at the time) Mark, while he was going to school in Austin. He had a really rundown apartment which was what he could afford at the time. The location was far south across from an HEB on Slaughter Lane. The first day I set foot in the apartment I felt a really negative and dark energy. The squeaky wooden floors made this place even creepier. I tried to cope before odd things started happening. The first night sleeping there I woke up to someone tugging on my feet then pulling on my pillow. Mark said I was imagining things, and he told me to just go back to bed. I tossed and turned the entire night. I was afraid. I could see a dark shadow in the room moving from the doorway to the window. I did not want to wake up Mark, or he would think I was big baby. I finally managed to fall asleep.

Suddenly Mark wakes me up at around 3 am. He asked "why is the window open? It's freezing in here. " I told him I thought he had gotten hot and opened it. He gave me an ugly look and shut the window and went back to sleep without saying another word. The next morning I woke up early to make my boyfriend breakfast and coffee before he went off to school. I went to wake him to let him know breakfast was ready. When we came to the kitchen the coffee pot was empty, and there was a large coffee stain on his kitchen wall. Confused by this we had an argument. He thought I was trying to run him out of his apartment, so he would come back home with me. He went off to school upset leaving the breakfast on the table.

Afraid to stay behind on my own, I got dressed and was headed out the door when an older lady standing just outside the door approached me and said "child, this is a dark dark place. You have no business in a fire like this. Go while you still can. " Then she walked away. As I turned to lock the door, I saw the curtain at the window just to the left of the door move slightly to one side, and a lady appeared to be peeking out from inside the apartment. I met up with my boyfriend and tried to explain what the older lady told me and what I saw. He did not bother to give me a chance before he broke it off with me and sent me on my way back home. I tried to give him some space. When I tried to contact him I got a nurse from a mental hospital; she said he had been hospitalized due to depression. I never heard from him again.

Submitted by Franchesca, Austin, Texas

. . . .

40.

At Peace At Home

Lindale, Texas

I have lived in Lindale, Texas about twenty years now. A few years back I came across some land that had an old house and an apartment on it, and I felt like I needed to live here. Funny thing is I lived a few blocks from it for years and never knew it was there because it was well hidden. One day I went to see some friends that lived close to it, and one of my friends asked me "why don't you buy the haunted house?" I said "what haunted house?" She said "let's go look at it. " So I jumped right on that deal. We went up a long drive way, and I went to see the house. As I walked in the door, there was a woman's voice said "how much more do I have to take?" I said back to the woman after knowing what she was talking about. Kids had torn her house up. I said "no honey. I want to buy the house and fix it back up. "

I found the owner, and it was his mother's house. She had passed. I would call him. I was trying to tell him I really wanted the land. He finally gave in and told me yes. I would go over there every day for a long time trying to decide how to fix the house. Then I got busy in my everyday life and stopped going for a while, but each time I went there I would take pictures. I would go home and put them on my computer. I would go to the land by myself, but in the pictures I saw people. Some was dressed in long dresses and bonnets and other Amish style. I could even see dogs and other stuff in my pictures.

Well I have been living there for about a week now, and I feel so much as home there. It is so peaceful, but I know my family is not the only ones there. I see things like people walking by and all. However, all in all I am at peace there.

Submitted by Lisa Marie, Lindale, Texas

. . . .

41.
Was It A Ghost?
North Tonawanda, New York

Growing up in North Tonawanda on Robinson Street, near Vandervoot, in a very old house heated by steam radiators, strange noises were often ignored. However one time, and only one time, I had seen with my own eyes a ghost walking past my bedroom. There were three bedrooms on the upper floor of the house, and I always kept my door open when I slept. Hearing the stairs creak, I assumed that my dad was walking up the stairs going to his bedroom, but he did not turn on the hallway light.

The steps came closer and closer to my room, which was across the hall from my parent's room. I was not afraid until what I saw next. No lights were on, but a glowing white human-shaped figure was standing and looking at me in my bed. It emitted a strange white light illuminating a human shape, but it made no sound. I screamed at the top of my lungs, and it turned and ran away, making no sound at all.

My mom and dad ran to my room, finding me shaking with fear. For years I slept with the light on in my room and then with the light on in the hallway. I never saw this again, and hope that I never will again. Was it a ghost? I really do not know. I may have been asleep, and everything that I saw was from a dream.

Years later my dad was outside shoveling snow when he saw my mom standing in the outside doorway. He said something to her, but she did not reply. Eventually he came in to find my mom asleep.

She never was standing by the door and had been asleep the entire time. The house that I grew up in was built by my great uncle. It had an apartment in the back where my dad and his mom lived. My uncle moved out of the house, and eventually my dad inherited the house and moved in. Our family lived there our entire lives, and my mom still lives there.

Submitted by NT Resident 1960s to 1970s, North Tonawanda, New York

. . . .

42.

Nixon

Austin, Texas

First off I'm just a southern Texas boy. I grew up out on my Grandparents' ranch in the Rio Grande Valley. I rounded up cows, took them out to the pastures and all that good stuff. Had a great dog, I named him Nixon. Anyhow my grandparents sent me out here to Austin to help out a great uncle and spend a summer out here. Trying something different for a change was good. I was 16 at the time. Great uncle Neil had tons of land and there was tons of wooded area around his property. Neil only had pigs and with Nixon's help the job was a breeze. We were done in no time so we had a lot of free time to go fishing and hunting on his land.

This happened one summer day going out fishing on my own at Slaughter Creek. I was walking a trail through the wooded area that gets you to perfect fishing spot. We had been exploring. Nixon and I'd been coming out to the creek for several days now having lots of luck catching largemouth and catfish. Best summer of my life so far. This time walking into the woods with Nixon was different. From a distance a dark image appeared to be floating and swaying back and forth on the trail. When Nixon barked this dark image turned around sporting deep burning red eyes. The image was there for a few seconds then quickly disappeared into thin air. This dark image appeared to have a white glowing orb around its entire body. I wasn't going to let that thing spook me.

I tried to walk in when Nixon started barking and backing up towards me pushing me back. I'd never encountered such a thing. He'd never done this. C'mon Nixon if you're not coming I'm going in without you. Suddenly a loud aggressive growl sounded deep in the distance. All the birds that were around flew out of the woods. A couple of deer scampered off. This time I felt a dark dark negative energy. This thing was too far to see but whatever it was

90

it was deeper in the thicker and heavier brush. Only it was now on my right side it had gotten closer to us. Nixon Continued to growl and bark at this thing.

As Nixon continued to bark you could hear this thing coming at us through the thick brush breaking branches and all. Nixon continued to bark and growl pushing me out of the trail. Suddenly Nixon bit my left leg and tugged for me to come out of the trail. He ran off towards the house and so did I. I told my uncle Neil and he didn't believe me, he said I shouldn't be spreading rumors. Neil took away all the guns he'd allowed me to use. He said I was becoming a liability. Boy had I screwed things up for myself here. He insisted that I either get a job in the city and help pay for bills or move back to my grandparents.

I picked up a part time job at Academy, in two pay checks I saved enough for my own 22 rifle, got an older buddy of mine Jimmy from work to get it for me. I'd talked to Jimmy about the incident in the woods with Nixon and me. We'd planed to go out there early one morning before my uncle would wake up. We took a few steps into the trail when Nixon goes off again barking like crazy and starts pushing back against us. This time Nixon ran into the woods so we proceeded to follow him deep into the woods. He stopped when we approached what looked like a small cemetery with 3 small tombstones. Nixon was quiet and we were looking around the area. When suddenly we heard several small footsteps coming at us, as well as the sound of the laughter of a few small children. We ran out of those woods faster than a bat outta hell. I parted ways with Uncle Neil and moved back to the Rio Grande. I still keep in touch with Neil, Jimmy and a few friends from work. I know there's something Neil knows about those haunted woods near his home. As I grew older I always thought of going back... One day I'll move to Austin and start my own ranch.

Submitted by Chad, Austin, Texas

. . . .

43.

The Spirit Of A Young Boy
University Place, Washington

While living in an apartment near Chamber Bay Golf Course I experienced many events. One day while sitting on the couch in the living room, suddenly all the doors in the hallway slammed shut at the same time. No windows or doors were opened to the outside, and no draft was present in the home. It was not possible for the doors to slam shut on opposite sides of the hallway. On another occasion I entered the apartment and set my keys on the kitchen counter, as I enter the doorway and went to the back bedroom to take off my shoes. When I returned, the keys were missing from the counter and were found on the dining room table. This happened often.

On many occasions I had overheard our daughter talking to someone while in her bedroom. This was when there were no cell phones. I knew there was no one else in her room and had just thought she was talking to herself, as some kids do when they are alone and want someone to talk to. I did not think anything of it at the time.

On another night I was asleep when I was awakened by my wife who was sleeping at my side. She had reached over to me and grabbed me violently. I awoke quickly and looked over at her and asked what was going on. She looked up at me with fear in her eyes, and she was grasping her neck and gasping for air. In the darkness I could see a haze over her and the outline of something on top of her, apparently trying to choke her. I got up and swung into the air above her and screamed that in the name of Jesus Christ leave our home. Suddenly our daughter came in and whatever was on top of my wife left.

Days after this incident, we invited a friend over who was a clairvoyant. We did not tell her why we invited her over, only that she was invited for dinner. When she arrived at the door she paused and then announced that she knew why we invited her and to not say anything and wait for her in the living room. She immediately went to our daughter's bedroom. She spent some time in there then went across the hall to our bedroom. After another short time she came back out and sat down next to my wife and me. She proclaimed that there were two spirits in the apartment. One roamed the grounds of the apartment complex, and the other was concentrating on my wife.

She explained that our daughter has communicated with the roaming spirit, and it was the spirit of a young boy that just liked to play jokes by moving things and seemed to be a guardian against the other spirit. The other spirit was evil and knew my wife and had blamed her for his torment. It appeared to have been her father who had abused her as a child, and he was sent to prison. He had recently passed away. The night of the choking incident our daughter was talking with the boy spirit, so he was not able to stop the evil spirit until our daughter came into the room with him. She had said that the evil spirit would not bother us anymore since the boy spirit had made his presence known.

Knowing that, we all settled into knowing that we were protected by the boy spirit and stopped fearing the spirit. One day while I was showering with the lights on, and no one else was in the apartment, suddenly the lights turned off. I thought it was the boy spirit playing, so I said to him "Haha, I know it's you playing a joke, you got me. Can you please turn the light back on, so I can finish taking my shower?" No sooner had I asked that question, the lights turned back on. I then thanked him.

Submitted by Scott, University Place, Washington

. . . .

44.

Our Visitor

I have been "followed" by something for many years as my family would say. At first I did not want to conclude it was a "ghost" and would often reason whatever the occurrence was away as our imagination running wild. I would find a reasonable explanation for whatever it was that caused us concern. Until I started to have concrete happenings that even with all of my attempts to find reason I could not explain. So, instead I started to leave it in God's hands and when they would happen I would just pray on it and ask God to keep my family and myself healthy, happy, and safe.

Then over a year ago we moved into a house in Los Altos. I grew up in Long Beach, and after years of living in Orange County I was so excited to be back in Long Beach. I finally felt home again. About three months into my family of four living here we started having weird things happening. I think I was the first, but for the sake of my young children I kept it to myself. Then after my young sister moved in with us, the entire atmosphere in the house changed. My children were now having strange occurrences and becoming more and more upset about them. Some of the more common things were lights turning on and off, doors opening and closing, growling noises being heard, feelings of someone watching them. All of the text book things that you would read about.

I have kept a firm hand and tried to comfort them by saying it has some kind of logical explanation. However, the worst of all is our "visitor. " We have on many occasions seen a man around thirty standing or walking around our front door at night. We have even had knocking, and the door bell rang. When we open the door there is nothing there. We have even gone as far as called the police because it is so real. Then my four-year-old daughter started to see a man inside the house. She refers to him as "the

94

man" and will at random times tell us that the man is in the room or looking at us. She describes him as white, tall, over weight with black hair and "eyes like mommy's. " She does not at all seem scared by him. When she sees him it is more matter of fact than a fearful thing.

Part of me is very worried by this, and part of me is very curious because my father passed away at the age of fifty while I was pregnant with her. He was so excited for her. I had no idea what the gender of my child was at the time, but he was certain it was a girl and was planning for her. Unfortunately he passed in November, and she was born in April. The man she described was to the tee the description of my father. I have asked my landlord, and he said that he has never had any experiences (he raised his family in the home) or heard of any in the home. Who knows who it is visiting my daughter. I do believe there is more than one entity here in this house in Los Altos.

Submitted by Jenn, Long Beach, California

. . . .

45.

Still There Watching

Warminster, Pennsylvania

I grew up in Warminster, but the strangest experience was when I was six. When I was little I was scared to sleep alone. So, of course, my parents improvised. I had to sleep alone, but I could have the hallway light on with my bedroom door open, and my father would turn it off when I was asleep. It was the second week of when my first experience happened. I woke up in the middle of the night, why? I did not know. I was a heavy sleeper. The only way to wake me was to scream my name. I was half asleep when I noticed that the hallway light was still on. By the window outside, I could tell it was around midnight already. My father would never leave that light on. He is cheap like that.

I heard someone whisper my name. I, at the time, believing it was my father. I waited, but I heard nothing. Then, as I was about to fall back to sleep, I saw a figure standing in the doorway. It was of a girl. I had no sisters. She looked around eleven or twelve. She had straight hair that was dirty blonde, a grayish-white dress on, and smiled as she saw me. Though I noticed that with each passing second, her smile would get darker. One of those smiles that you knew held a secret, and from then on I and my family's life seemed to get harder. Me being a scared six-year-old, I hid under my blanket and chanted in my head "it's not real. It's not real. " After that I never saw her again.

Though I never saw her after that, things just never felt right. It felt like someone was always looming over you. I was always scared to be alone in the house sometimes. After her I witnessed a man standing on the side of my bed. As I looked at him, he was wearing all black with a hood covering his head and face. He just stood there not moving.

In the morning my mother claimed to have heard someone saying her name that night and choked her. The thing though, was that when my mother was a child, she would see a man in a cloak. Later when I was ten, I saw a boy in my house. He appeared to be about the same age as me. He just sat on our carpet and stared at the floor. You could hear mumbling coming from him. That night, my brother claimed to have seen an old man with a top hat and knife.

Now as I reflect on my experiences, I noticed that the younger I was, the more things would happen. I also noticed that most of them happened when I was alone, and no one else was in the house. Sometimes even with the bad spirits lurking, a few spirits would make me feel safe from them. Like the boy. Soon things lightened up in my family again, but it always felt like they were still there watching.

Submitted by Samantha, Warminster, Pennsylvania

46.

Old Hospital

Belton, Texas

Around 1985 there was an old hospital that had been turned into apartments. The building had a reputation of ghosts because it had been a hospital for years and many people died there. My boyfriend (Larry) at that time rented the top floor of the building that had been the operating room at one time. It had a large skylight in the middle of the ceiling that was now the living room but had been the operating room long ago. Of course they did not have the lighting we have today, so skylights and windows were necessary. There was an old elevator that was still in use and came right up to the operating room, plus a stairway right next to it.

One morning Larry called me and asked me to come over and see something. When I came into the living room he pointed to the wall under the windows. Neatly lined up against the wall were the contents of his pants pockets. His change was lined up one coin next to the other, his comb, billfold, as well as his nail clippers. The money was all in his billfold, so no one had robbed him. Larry said he had slept on the couch and awakened to see his pockets contents over against the wall.

One night while I was there we were in the bedroom discussing the possibility of ghosts there, and all of a sudden we heard the crystals on an antique lamp begin to start spinning very fast. There was no breeze and no open windows, but the crystals were spinning so fast. We went into the room, and it was very cold in the room. I began to talk to whatever entity it was and said "whatever happened to you in this room was long ago, and now you have gone on into another dimension. It is a different time. You are not a part of this time anymore. " The crystals stopped swinging.

98

The man who owned the apartment house showed us some pictures he took while remodeling of that room, and there was a misty figure in the door way, but there was no human standing in the door way. In one of the apartments below this there was a couple who moved because they said night after night they would hear a cat screaming in the closet, or something that sounded like a cat, but when they looked nothing was there. Larry was not scared but moved after about three months of this. I would have moved the first day.

Submitted by Mary, Belton, Texas

. . . .

47.

At The Gym

Holyoke, Massachusetts

I was working at Holyoke Community College for six years in the fitness center. Every time I walked in the front door my coworkers would always talk to me and the other coworkers of mine of what has been going on there. The janitor told me that when she came in at 4:00 am to clean the locker rooms she could hear water running in the showers, but when she went back there to check it out no one was there, but the water was still on full blast and running. One day I was locking up for the night. I went around to see if all the doors were locked, and I went to the back stairwell on the second floor. When I did I heard footsteps coming up the stairs toward the second floor. I said "hello. " No one was there. After that happened I heard what sounded like a flat bed pushcart dragging across the floor downstairs in the Janitor room.

Then one other day in the summer time my coworker and I were in the front desk office talking. All of a sudden we both heard a big banging noise on the wall across from the front desk door. We both jumped up out of our seat and went to investigate the hallway. That was where we heard the banging noise, and as soon as we got out to the hallway it stopped. However, when we went back into the front desk office it started banging on the wall again.

One other day in December 2011 I was in the gymnasium in the morning time around 7 am. I was cleaning the floor. I was the only person in there, and no one else was around. I then heard a man's voice. It said "you're fired," and then soon after that I heard a woman's voice saying "hi. " I looked around and did not see anybody. I then ran out of the gymnasium and told my coworker that something was really going on in this place. I told her what had just happened. She did not want to believe me, but I know it was true because I witnessed it.

One night I was locking up again in November 2011 at 9:00 pm closing time. I was going to the locker rooms to shut off the lights. Before I did that I hollered out and said "is there anyone in here? Because we are shutting down now for the night. " As soon as I said that a woman's voice called out and said "Hello. " There was no one in there at all. It was totally empty.

Submitted by Dennis, Holyoke, Massachusetts

. . . .

48.

There Was Nothing There

Vinemont, Alabama

I live in a house almost a hundred years old in Vinemont. We have had several strange things happen here. About two weeks after we moved in around 10 o'clock we heard someone run up the stairs. We were watching TV, and the movie was really intense. We both looked at each other and one of us said "It must be our daughter coming in from her date. " Then we said" but it's early for her, I'll check on her when the movie goes off. " In a few minutes the movie was over, and I ran upstairs and called her name. No one was there. We both heard this. It was pretty loud. My husband did not believe in ghosts and still will not talk about it.

On one occasion, I was drying my hair with my head upside down. I heard someone walk up to me over the noise of the hair dryer. I turned it off and expected it to be my husband. I asked "what did you forget?" No one was there. It was someone with rubber or work boots on I was sure. They walked right up to me and stopped. We know this used to be an old farm house. It was part of a hundred-acre farm.

I have seen fog like figures that hovered and moved from one side of the room to the other. Our cat would sit on our table and stare at the ceiling. She would move her head and meow like she was following something. It would give me the creeps, so I would make her move. She would not go upstairs.

My daughter who lived upstairs at the time always felt like something was up there. She reported things moving from where she would put them at night. She said her jacket would always be lying on the floor the next morning. She knew she laid it on her chair. Things would fall off her shelf for no reason. A toy that was given to her by a friend six years earlier suddenly fell on the floor

102

one day. She picked it up and placed it back on the shelf. It came on and spoke to her saying "that's funny". The battery was corroded, and the toy was not turned on. She threw it away. Shortly after this she moved.

I have been awakened in the middle of the night by voices or old music coming from upstairs. I would lie there too scared to go check it out because I knew there was nothing there.

Submitted by Vicky, Vinemont, Alabama

. . . .

49.

A Hound From Hell

Lake Elsinore, California

From 1988 to 1993 I lived on W. Pottery St. My husband and I were thrilled to buy an old home that needed some renovation and TLC; it was built in the 1910s. Not long after moving in, my oldest daughter said the house had a ghost. She is a 'sensitive', a person who 'sees' spirits, so I did not doubt her. If our family was upstairs, we would hear footsteps on the wooden floors below, and vice versa. Occasionally we would wake up at night to the smell of pot roast, even though I had not cooked any. Once in a while a cabinet door would be open even though none of us had been in the room.

What really scared me to the core was hearing what could only be described as a 'hound from hell. ' I was up late one night scoring students' papers. My second story office had windows that faced the back yard. I heard some snarling, very low at first, and I thought it was our dog reacting to a possum. As the eerie snarling and growling grew louder, I knew it was not the dog. She had NEVER made such a sound. There was no way another dog could have gotten into the yard. The hair on my arms stood up, and I froze in fear. I wanted to awaken my husband and tell him to come and hear this demonic growling, but I could not move. This went on for about five minutes, and then the growling stopped.

We moved to Wildomar in 1993 and rented out the Pottery house for a couple of years. None of our tenants complained of unusual activity, but for some reason they would not live there long. I wonder if others who have lived there since had experiences too.

Submitted by Owlqueen, Lake Elsinore, California

. . . .

50.
Getting Attention

Corpus Christi, Texas

I went to a business place that is part of the company I work for last Easter Sunday about 5:45pm. I was told there were sounds of door slamming, pictures moving on the walls, and numerous other things that were happening consistent with a spirit being in the area. I went because these things were unnerving, and my friends were working there. I can "feel" a spirit's presence and sometimes see as well as hear them (since I was a child). I walked into the office building and just stood there for awhile. Then I walked to the areas where everything was happening. I told my friend I did not really feel any difference in the energy there and did not think there was a spirit there.

The supervisor came in, so I told them both I would take a few pictures of the office anyway since I was already there. I took eight or ten pictures with my phone. We all went to an area that had more light and ran through the pictures. After about the fifth picture a head showed up in several of them. It was a man with blue eyes that looked either scared or shocked. They glared at us. I decided that it could have been a picture in that office I accidentally got pictures of, so I walked down a long hallway to a door (closed) and took six more pictures. There was nothing between me and the door, but when I ran through the six pictures there was the same head, so I believe that spirit was there trying to get our attention. I must say it sure did that. I will be going back this Easter to see if he is still there.

Submitted by Mandy, Corpus Christi, Texas

51.

My House

Huffman, Texas

I have been a Huffman resident for over 30 years. We live in a very rural setting on the East Fork of the San Jacinto River. My wife and I built our house about 23 years ago on raw land after it was cleared.

About 18 years ago I experienced an older man and a young girl walking through our living room late at night. I had been asleep on the couch while watching TV when out of nowhere this man dressed in what looked like a suit which might have been worn in the 1800s walked through with a young girl of about 5 or 6 dressed in a dress of the same era.

I thought I might have been experiencing a waking dream but I looked over at our pet dog Brutus, a boxer who was staring at the exact spot where the apparitions appeared. These same apparitions appeared numerous times over the next few years and at times you could hear the little girl laughing quietly as if she were playing.

My wife being a little upset began salting the corners of our house and smudging sage throughout the house and the encounters ceased as quickly as they had begun. One day I went wandering through the woods next to our house and found an old houseplace that I never knew existed.

There were the remains of old wooden support blocks and 4 ancient oak trees that were located as if they specifically had been planted to shade the houseplace from the western sun. I somehow believe that these apparitions lived there and may have died from an early flood of the river.

Submitted by Gary, Huffman, Texas

. . . .

52.
He Was So Fun

Eagle Butte, South Dakota

When I was like six or seven I went to a carnival. I do not really remember where we were and never talked about it, but it was almost by my home town Eagle Butte. Anyway, what I remember was that we were camping out because we were also attending a powwow. We only camped out for two days, and on the last day my mom let me go run around the carnival. I do not remember how I met this other boy my age. We ran around the carnival and powwow together. He was fun, so I played with him. He had torn up shoes and kind of hairy legs for a little boy (ha-ha) and a green shirt with a couple of holes in it. He had black straight hair that was not braided.

We got on all the carnival rides for free. He and I just got on any carnival ride we wanted. Then when everything was over, and everyone was going home the boy said "is it time for you to go home?" I looked at him, and I said "yes but I'm waiting for my mom to call me over. " The boy said "now I'm just going to have my mom and my dad. " I did not know what he meant, so I did not say anything. By then my mom called me over, and I did not want to leave either. The boy looked at me, so I said "don't you have to go home? Where do you live?" He looked like he was going to cry, so I told him I have to go now and started walking away. The boy said "there's my mom!" I looked behind me, and I saw him run into the trees, and there was nobody out there! It was pitch black by the trees.

Submitted by D'shaun Star E.C., Eagle Butte, South Dakota
. . . .

107

53.

In The Projects

Havre De Grace, Maryland

Back in 1980 in the projects we lived on Wilson Street. My husband and I were in bed and in the semi darkness the street light was shining a little through the curtains. From the closet drifted a solid black figure shaped like Charlie Brown. It turned and looked toward us, and where the eyes would have been were two darker than its black form eyes looking at us. No other feature was there. It was just a pitch black figure. It continued slowly drifting past and then to the corner of the room and was gone. My husband leaped out of bed and ran outside to see where it went, and nothing was there.

A month later each time I went to the kitchen sink something would run loudly up behind me and stop dead at my heels. I would turn around, and nothing was ever there. After several more times I told my husband who laughed it off and said it was air in the pipes. I told him "go to the sink. Put your hands in there and push around a few dishes. Don't turn on the water. " (I found this out that morning when it happened to me.) It ran up behind him like it had done to me. We moved out a few weeks later when we had enough money to go. I heard the homes were taken down later, but it was a creepy event in our lives. We figured maybe a kid with water on the brain may have lived and eventually died there once.

Submitted by Melanie, Havre De Grace, Maryland

. . . .

54.
Old Chief

Blythe, California

I had a mobile home along Hwy 95 at Water Wheel Resort about twenty-five miles north of Blythe between Blythe and Parker, Arizona. This was back in 1998 to 1999. I was working on my trailer and needed some material one afternoon, so I headed to Parker. I pulled out of the resort headed north on Hwy 95 a few miles down before Lost Lake Resort. Then I came up along a hill, and on the side of the road looking right at me as I drove by was an old Indian chief in full head dress with feathers from head to toe. He looked like what I have seen in old pictures of what Indian chiefs wore. In that split time our eyes met.

I will never forget how it was so clear. As I went by, in my mind I said to myself "that wasn't what I thought, was it?" I turned around to see, and there was no one. I know how strange it sounds because I have never believed in ghosts. However, I know what I saw, and there was nowhere for anyone to hide. I could see how old the man looked, so he could not have hidden. I will never forget how real he was. I will always remember him looking at me like he was staring into my eyes. It was weird but honest truth. I have never been able to forget, and I am sure I never will.

Submitted by Dave, Blythe, California

. . . .

55.
A Farmer With Overalls

Dalton, Georgia

I moved with my parents from Kentucky to Dalton, GA back in 1997. We rented a nice house on Beaverdale Road. Upon living there for about a month we started hearing faint whispers on the baby monitors, so my dad unplugged them brushing it off as malfunction. The next encounter was when we came home one night, and my mom saw an older man wearing overalls and a red shirt on our back porch. He was looking at us. However, none of us saw this but her, and it really freaked her out.

Another time was when my mom was at work. I was using the bathroom. When I stood up I saw the old man standing there looking at me. He turned. As he walked away, he just disappeared. It scared me so bad I went and stayed with friends till my parents came home. I have seen the same man as my mom. On another occasion the hair dryer came on by itself. I was telling this to my friends at school when one of the girls said her grand dad was killed in our yard. She said he was a farmer, and all he wore was overalls and flannel shirts. My mom burned candles, and we said a prayer for him. We were never bothered again.

Submitted by Ashley, Dalton, Georgia

. . . .

56.
The Three-Knock

Jourdanton, Texas

When my siblings and I were little we lived in a house on Willow Street. There was a shadow of a man that would go from room to room, but he would be on the wall. When he would come to a corner, he would bend with the corner and continue. We were always scared to live there. My eldest sister would always sleep by the window, being the eldest, and she would hear breathing. It was scary. We grew up and moved away. The house and land had been sold. Many years went by, and I would notice that all kinds of people would move in and out. Then finally they knocked down the house and put a mobile home there. Well, that is gone too. It makes me wonder what is really there.

About six years ago my brother asked me if I would go stay the night with him at his house, and I said yes. He had warned me that his ex-wife would always hear three solid knocks outside her bedroom window, and then she would see a dark see-through shadow come in her room. When it would go in front of the fan, the fan would stop blowing air because there was an object or something in front stopping it. Anyhow, I said I would. That night I was sitting on the floor reading some kind of biblical scripture. I was not scared; I know that Jesus is my savior and stronger than anything in this world. Well, I heard the three- knock on the window frame. They were solid and one right after the other. I listened and thought maybe it was my brother playing a joke, but I could hear him talking on the phone and laughing in the other room. I started to pray, and then I rebuked it in Jesus name. I sat there; I did not move, and I did not let it bother me. Well, I did not hear it again that night.

I was sleeping on the floor, and in front of me was the big dresser. In front of the window was the night stand, and behind me was the bed. I told my brother to make sure and get on and of the bed

111

at the end of the foot of the bed, so he would not step on me. During the night, and I cannot say what time it was, I felt someone walking around me. I was in between sleep and being awake, but I know it was because one time I said "don't step on me. " I was more awake that time. I felt this thing walking around me. At the same time I was too lazy to open my eyes, and I nodded off again. In the morning I asked my brother what he was doing walking around me. He said he never did. He fell asleep and did not wake up at all that night. He moved out and sold the place. I believe that house is no longer there; it is gone.

Another time I was renting a house by the Pleasanton Jr. High. There was this old couple living there before. The poor man died, and the sweet old lady rented the house to us. It was all fine until one day. At 10:00 pm on the dot the television in our bedroom would always turn off. It never failed from that time on. It was the TV that belonged to the little old couple. However, that did not frighten me. I thought "wow!" Then my girls would ask me if I was up sewing late at nights, and I said no. They said they would always hear the sewing machine going every night. I used to leave it on the table, up and ready to go. Then one day no one was home. I came home, and it was late at night. The front door was open, and it was dark. I went in and looked down the long dark hall, called out, and found nothing. I looked in the kitchen, and we had an old metal stool by the garage door in the kitchen. We were in the process of putting new floor, so the kitchen floor was just concrete. I went to the bedrooms, and then I heard the stool screeching as it was moving from one side of the wall to the other. I hauled it out the door. I noticed that when my stepmom bought me a couch, our troubles started soon after that. Coincidence or what? I do not know, and that is just a few I can tell you. My Grandpa had some stories he could tell and they are very interesting.

Submitted by Alice, Jourdanton, Texas

. . . .

57.

Sharing The Home

Owego, New York

During a time about 2 years ago, I lived in a lovely large downstairs apartment near St. Pat's Church on Main Street in Owego. I was well aware of hauntings in Owego as well as in my apartment from firsthand experience. I lived there with no one else but my loyal pussycat, Thumper.

During one dark and late evening I was tucked well and cozy under my plump down comforter sitting up watching TV. The television was elevated on a stand against the wall past the foot of my bed. My cat sat at my left side in the large four-poster bed we happened to be sharing as we did often. I would speak to her, and if you are a cat fancier you know that having a conversation with your pet is not out of the norm. I was watching a really good movie. My cat though was disinterested and laid with her tail curled around her wrapping her up into a purring bundle of fur as her eyes were thin slits.

As I was distracted with the movie I sensed a tugging at my feet. At first I did not feel concern because I have had this occur as my Thumper would play while I wiggled a blanket. I then focused on the moment at hand and looked to see if my kitty had jumped off the bed and was doing her usual game playing with me. Whoa! I looked at that cat beside me, and she was up in a sitting position intent on whatever was at the foot of my bed. She, just as I, could not see what was on the floor tugging on my bedding, but we both saw that the bedding was moving. I then noticed a pressure mark like the weight of some small being was putting a hand, a paw, a finger, or small foot down on my quilted cover way at the foot of my bed. What was more unnerving was that it was moving progressively forward toward me and my cat. I could not believe what I was seeing but realized when I looked at my cat something

113

very weird was happening, and she was watching each spot as new pressure was applied.

While taking a moment to concentrate on slowing my speeding heart and rapid breathing, I then took action. I stated in a firm but quiet slow voice "I am not sure what you are doing here, but you are welcome to stop right there and be still. You can stop and relax or watch this movie with us but share this space with us. " Oh MY goodness! The pressure marks just lifted to smoothness. The weight on my feet from the comforter being pulled just let go. I experienced nothing new as I stayed another six-month period, but I left to go to another place with a heavy heart as I felt akin to whatever or whoever the entity was that shared space with us.

Submitted by Susan, Owego, New York

. . . .

58.

In The Basement

Alpena, Michigan

I lived in an apartment on the north side of Apena. It was a house over 100 years old, on one of the oldest streets. I would hear voices, those of my boyfriend who was not home, or ones I did not recognize. Breathing would start right in my ear, loud, and I would turn, and it would move away from me. I could follow it around the apartment and back into a corner, and it would disappear and start up behind me again. I would hear (I thought) my boyfriend come in, take his shoes off, walk in to the kitchen, and open the cupboards and fridge. I would be in the computer room where I could not see into the kitchen or anything. I would call his name, and everything would go silent. I would walk out, and no one was there, and the door was locked. It started getting really scary.

We both had night terrors, and he had really bad "attacks" at night, feeling and sometimes seeing a misty presence that would make him feel like it was taking his energy and holding him down. I woke up a few times feeling that. We both woke up feeling that. One night he was facing my back. I could not move, so I could not see anywhere but straight in front of me. I did not even know he was awake too. When I could finally move he sat up freaking out and said there was a brown blob of smoky looking stuff spinning above me, while we were both awake and paralyzed. The basement always felt evil. There were two occasions where friends witnessed a large shadow in our window which was four feet off the ground. It was reaching all the way to the top, and it was a five-foot tall window. When we went outside to see if someone was out there, there were not even footprints in the snow.

Another huge shadow took up our whole driveway one night. We thought it was just dark there because it was night time, but all of a sudden the whole huge shadow in the drive way moved to the left and was gone. The driveway was lit by the streetlight after it moved. The light was not flickering and was on the entire time. I blessed the house, and my neighbor (the house is split into several apartments) called me a few days later. She told me a bunch of things she was experiencing that were exactly like what we went through. I think it moved to her apartment. That was the worst place I have ever lived. I moved not soon after that. I think something bad happened there. In the basement I could feel it.

Submitted by Resident, Alpena, Michigan

. . . .

59.
Something Is Very Wrong

San Angelo, Texas

When I was a child we lived in a rent house on Buchanan which runs parallel to Florence. So much stuff happened there, but we always found ways to rationalize or dismiss the things we saw or heard. Supposedly some man had been stabbed to death there before we moved in, but I have never researched and confirmed that. We lived there for about seven years. After we moved out that house went through so many different tenants, and most would not last six months. Then it became abandoned. I am sure while it was vacant people went in there and did things because walls and windows were broken, and at one point it was boarded up. Then someone bought it, and my brother inquired about renting it.

One day I decided to stop by and visit "our childhood home". I walked in to the kitchen first and immediately got a creepy feeling. I did not say anything because I had my seven-year-old with me. Then we walked into the living room and then what used to be my brother's room. As soon as I walked in there I had to step back. I could not even walk into what used to be my bedroom. I got a sense of urgency to get out. I immediately turned and told my brother "I have to get out of here. I feel very strange. Something is wrong here!" I grabbed my son very close and walked quickly out of the house. As I was walking to get out of the house, I thought I was going to stop breathing. I kept telling my brother and his girlfriend "I can't be in here. Something is very wrong, and I don't know what it is!" Once we were outside his girlfriend asked me what was wrong. I said "I don't know but look at the hair standing up on my arms. She looked at my brother and said "should we tell her?" I asked "tell me what?"

Then my brother told me that whatever was in that house sometimes it would be so bad they would go to a hotel. He said his neighbor also was experiencing abnormal things next door. My jaw dropped. I was so upset they were still living there. They had two kids, and I told him "you better move before something really bad happens. " They moved out a few weeks later. The house has remained vacant since.

Submitted by Anonymous, San Angelo, Texas

. . . .

60.

A British Soldier

Norwalk, Connecticut

I live in Norwalk, and the cemetery behind Lockwood Mathews Mansion is haunted. I had recently moved into the neighborhood and did not know the place quite well. Late October coming home from work late, I asked a friend to show me the way home. We both walked toward Lockwood Mathews Mansion. It was very cold out, so we tried to find a shortcut home up to Butler Street. We quickly walked through the grounds at the mansion, climbed the stone wall, and went through the cemetery about 11pm in the evening. We slowly walked along the wall. A few minutes later I heard a whistle. I asked my friend if he was whistling a soft song as he walked. He had said "No," so we stopped and looked around. We saw a British soldier with a tripod hat and uniform walking down the cemetery path. My friend said something to me, and I said someone was playing a joke. Then we walked a little farther, and the solider just looked at us and evaporated into thin air. There was not even a breeze. We ran the length of the path without stopping to the main gate and ran all the way home. Later I realized I had lost my eyeglasses and my work apron. My friend said I must have dropped them running.

The next day we went back to the cemetery to see if I had left them there, and they were neatly folded and placed on the tombstone in the center of the cemetery. We noticed a hand was placed on shoulder, and no one else was there. We heard the same whistling we heard the night before. To this day we believe we saw a British soldier from the colonial era watching over the grounds. We have returned time and time again, but we have never seen him. As we did research on the cemetery we found that British soldiers stood watch at night and kept their horses tied to the gates.

Submitted by Wayne, Norwalk, Connecticut

61.
You Will Pull Through

Bay City, Michigan

As a teenager I used to hang around at cemeteries since Bay City really doesn't have much for a teenager to do. I will tell you my story of Oak Ridge Cemetery. All this began in 2004. As do most teens and children who have troubled families, we do our best to avoid our houses. I mostly hung out in abandoned places or cemeteries. After a few nights of being there I meet the current caretaker. After a few conversations he had given permission to stay there past dusk. He just asked me to never sleep there, which I never did. He knew I was not a threat. He always saw me cleaning up graves or fixing them.

One night I stayed past dusk lost in my own thought. Then this older man and woman were walking their dog right beside me and my car. The older man had asked me why a young lady such as myself was out in the cemetery so late. I explained family troubles. The older woman stated to me "you are strong. You will pull though sweetie. One day at a time. " At this time I decided it was best to go home. I did not want random people to worry about me. We said goodbye.

When I looked back at them, I noticed that they no longer had legs and were pretty much turning into a mist. Then they started to move away at an extremely fast speed. I got in my car to drive around and find them, but there was no trace of them. I was shocked, however not scared. I never saw them again when I would stay late.

Submitted by Kai, Bay City, Michigan

. . . .

62.
Brenda In The Pink Dress

Cohutta, Georgia

I was the aunt that was in the story about the little girl named Brenda in a pink dress. I was visiting my niece and her four kids. My mother was also there. I heard a voice saying "mommy, hey mom. " My mother and I looked at my niece and asked her if she was going to check and see what her oldest daughter wanted. She was the only one asleep in that way, but the voice was much younger sounding to me. I thought it was just me. When my niece opened the door to ask her daughter what she wanted she was sound asleep. We woke her up hollering at her. She rose up and told us to go out. She was not calling for us.

We all heard this small child's voice around the age of five to seven years old. My three-year-old niece continued to play with a girl named Brenda. She has also seen my dead husband whom she loves very much. She talked to him, looked up at the ceiling, and asked who the other man was with my dead husband. I think the unknown man was my dead father that my three-year-old niece had never met. This all took place in Cohutta, GA close to Saint Clairs and Midway Market.

The mobile home is haunted with good spirits so far though! Brenda still plays with my niece daily. They played house-and-dress-up today. My niece fixed them some fried chicken even in her little play kitchen set for supper one night. This story is so true of the little girl named Brenda in a pink dress. I have heard her myself!

Submitted by Aunt Nim, Cohutta, Georgia
. . . .

63.

In The Hallway

Murfreesboro, Tennessee

I lived in a house in Murfreesboro, TN for twenty-five years. I moved there when I was a junior in high school. This house was also near the Stones River Battlefield. In fact it was documented that there was a union bunker right near our backyard. While I was still in high school I would be studying in my room, and I would hear odd noises, and items would shift on my shelves. If I would say out loud "Not now. I have to study," It would stop. I would feel like someone was there sometimes late at night. As I was falling asleep, I would hear music even though no music was playing.

A few years later, my niece and nephew were about five or six and visiting my parents. They were running up and down the hallway playing. My niece came running into the living room laughing and said to her mom (my sister) "there's a man at the end of the hallway!" My sister played along and said "and just what does this man look like?" She smiled and said "he is wearing a blue suit that isn't a suit-suit... Like a soldier" Then she ran away to play. We looked at each other and came to the conclusion that she and her brother were not scared, so no worries! However, my sister went to the hallway and said just to be sure "you will leave my children alone. " No more issues for their visit! It was never an everyday thing, but it was from time to time something moving, turning on or off, and cats that were freaked out by the end of the hallway.

Submitted by Mickeybuny, Murfreesboro, Tennessee
. . . .

64.
Little Red Hood

Attica, Indiana

My wife and I just recently stayed at a hotel. It needs a much needed update, but then I have heard the stories about it being haunted and wanted to check it out. We went to bed around 11:00 pm. At midnight the room started to get brighter then dark and bright again, but it was not from any light source in the room. I looked out the windows, and there were no cars passing by. It happened again an hour later.

I rolled over to look at the room because I felt like someone was watching me. As I rolled all the way there was a young child in a red long coat with a hood over her head just standing and staring in front toward the room door. I yelled for my wife to look, but the young child was gone. My wife told me to shut up and go to bed. I buried my head under the covers and woke to the room getting brighter again. I rolled over and saw the same child with the red coat three feet from me.

I did not feel threatened but was scared. I flipped on the light, and she was gone. I did not feel anyone in the room after that. The next day we found the closet door had been opened. I asked my wife if she had any experiences, and she said she heard music and laughter in the middle of the night. I believe we were the only ones staying there that night, and the bar closed at 11:00 pm. Cool experience at the least.

Submitted by Jim, Attica, Indiana

. . . .

65.

Mini Man

Oxford, Pennsylvania

I was driving back to my home in Oxford, PA after babysitting on a foggy evening in June. The fog was fairly thick, and I could see no more than thirty feet ahead of me. I was minutes away from my house when all of a sudden a mysterious dark figure ran across the road in front of me. Standing at only four feet tall, it was a solid black color and appeared to be hunched over. His movement was a cross between running and a glide. Upon seeing the figure, I was instantly struck with a negative energy. To me it was a feeling of evil, and it made me burst into tears. I was absolutely terrified. When I arrived home I could not stop shaking or crying after feeling so disturbed.

When I told the story to my parents and described the mini devilish creature, they looked at each other and were familiar with what I had seen. They told me a story of a night a couple of years before where they both had seen a figure. It matched the description and feeling of what I had described to them. The sightings were both on a back road off of Route 10.

Since that night I have not seen the figure again, but just playing the memory back in my mind gives me goose bumps and a pit in my stomach. After the sightings my family has named him the "Mini Man."

Submitted by Maddie, Oxford, Pennsylvania

. . . .

66.
I Was Not Dreaming

Dayton, Kentucky

I grew up in a house in Dayton, KY on Tenth Street. I had seen many things in the house. There was a man I used to see in the basement. Even though I felt fear I somehow knew he was not there to hurt or harm me. The fear came from the upstairs. There were very dark images that would come up out of the floor. At night I would say a prayer in my bed to fall asleep, so I would not see them. At one point I was almost pulled out of my bed. I could not see what it was, but it had a hold of my ankle.

With my sister sleeping next to me I grabbed the bed post holding on for dear life. The bed was actually shaking from this thing pulling on me. I was yelling my sister's name for her to help me but she would not wake up. When I told my Mom and Dad about it they just blew it off as if I was dreaming. I was not dreaming. I knew what I saw. I knew what happened to me. No one could tell me any different. The family home was bought by a family member since my parents died. I still to this day experience things in that house. I try to stay away from the upstairs though.

Submitted by Sharon, Dayton, Kentucky
. . . .

67.

Mysterious House

San Benito, Texas

My girlfriend and I loved going to this little restaurant called Lally's in San Benito. The coffee was great and so was the breakfast. One morning we were looking through the paper trying to locate a place to rent while we saved up for the purchase of our own home. When an older couple that was sitting next to us overheard us talking and suggested we rent one of the homes that they own. They were letting us rent it out at a very affordable price. They handed over the key to the home and insisted that we go check it out at our convenience. We'd meet back up same place same time tomorrow. We could not pass off this offer. The home was beautiful. We were so grateful they were helping us out. Plus they wouldn't take no for an answer. We happily took their offer. Talk about being at the right place at the right time. It was our first year renting this house that was located on Jay St. Even though it was an old home it was beautiful. With one exception we did always think there was this odd smell to the home since we'd moved in. Nothing Fabreez and candles can't fix.

One night I was up late watching TV when I heard what sounded like a loud scream coming from a lady from one of the rooms upstairs. As I went up to observe, our cat Wiskers came running down the stairs like a bat out of hell. I checked the master bedroom and my girlfriend was asleep. In one of the rooms a cross on the wall had been turned upside down. And the sheets on the bed were down on the floor. Maybe the cat dropped the sheets but the upside down cross was something else. I kept this to myself. I removed the cross and stored it away in the closet. A few nights later the lights would flicker on and off. We had an electrician come check things out the next day and he said the home had recently been rewired so everything was looking perfectly fine. He said it may be your provider and besides that he said it passed the city inspection. He said there was nothing to be concerned about. That was that.

Different subject. Our door leading to the garage has a window with no curtain or blind. So you can see in and out. The day after the electrician had come by my girlfriend was doing laundry in the garage when she was startled by an older man walking over and locking the door leading to the garage his image disappeared as he walked off. As spooked as she was she didn't know if this was a prank or if it was real. She didn't get a clear look at his face but she did say it was more like a blur but his clothes appeared to be that of an older man.

Scared out of her mind she reached for a screwdriver from my toolbox in the garage. She said she called my cell then called the cops. Unfortunately I had run out of battery and I missed her call. Suddenly the washer went out and so did the lights. It was pitch black and now she was really panicking. When she thought to reach for the button to open the garage door it also would not function. Luckily I showed her how to use the manual release lift to the garage door and she made an escape that route.

When I came home she claimed she was locked out of the house and was terrified. She was pale at the face. I remember as I pulled up to the driveway I saw a fire truck. First thought was there was an electrical fire but she got out ok. There were cops and an ambulance. She was sitting at the ambulance crying. I sat with her and held her close till she was ok again. The paramedics asked me if she takes any medications or if she's mentally unstable. One medic said she seemed brain dead.

Their behavior was very upsetting to me, they were only making matters worse. The police men on duty said she claimed someone was in the home and she said the door was locked from the inside and when they went to try and open the front door it was unlocked. They were asking questions about her mental state.

They asked if I knew of her being on any kind of drugs. This was very disturbing but I patiently answered their questions. They said they did a full search of the home and nothing was out of the ordinary. They said all windows we're locked and also the back door was locked from the inside so no one could have exited either way.

By the time they went in the power had come back on. They gave her a number to call. For help, some kind of substance abuse hotline. That night was hell for both of us. We finally settled back in and I didn't leave her side for the next couple of days. When I'd go to work she'd go to her parents' house just to be safe. We tried to contact the landlords but the number they gave us is no longer in service. Something is strange about this home. We had more important things to worry about. The upcoming weekend was very important to us. Saturday was our 5 year anniversary and we were so excited and ready to celebrate this day together.

I remember I had worked the night shift the night before and it was now our anniversary and I was off from work so I woke up went to the couch and fell asleep with the TV on while my girl went off to do some shopping. When I got up to brush my teeth in the half bath downstairs I heard the front door open than I heard the shower going in our master bath. She was home and was so excited to spend the day with her. I could smell the scent of roses throughout. I started getting dressed. I had a surprise for her. I'd be taking her out for a nice meal than we'd escape to South Padre for the weekend...

So as I was fixing my tie in the mirror in the hallway I saw the figure of a man dash across the way. This just ran chills down my spine. Who's there I called out ? I went and searched for anyone in the house. I searched all of the downstairs rooms when I suddenly saw the same figure of that man walking quickly up the stairs. It was more of a blur, not a full figure. It's hard to explain since it happened so fast but it was a male for sure. I tried to catch up

128

before I heard a loud scream coming from our master bath he had gotten to my girlfriend.

My heart just sunk as I tried to run up the stairs, I froze in my tracks. I felt so helpless, what was happening? Why was this happening to us? As I stood there hearing the screams that's when I also heard the front door open. Finally I was able to make it upstairs. As I was looking around clasping onto a pair of scissors I heard my girlfriend's voice. Honey I'm home. I have a surprise for us ! I screamed wait outside babe! It's not safe!

What a relief she was ok. But who was upstairs taking a shower, who was that man and who was screaming. What was going on? I checked the master bedroom no one was there, I checked the master bath. The hot water in the shower had been running and the floor was wet. There on the condensated mirror was a written message. Reading "Your Are Not Alone!".

We packed a small bag and headed to my parents. Never did we go back... Nor do we intend to. The landlords we tried to contact were nowhere to be located. We talked to the neighbors and they said the landlords have been dead for quite a while. The neighbors across the street said horrible things have happened in that home and it's nothing to be messed with. So who were the people we spoke to and made arrangements with at the local coffee shop and restaurant? Does anyone have information or history to this home?

Submitted by Conrad, San Benito, Texas

. . . .

68.
Cleanse Your Home

Grove City, Ohio

It was October 23rd, 2010. My beautiful wonderful man was on a trip to the Nascar Martinsville Race. It was a Sunday evening, and he was expected home the following day. My daughters and I spent the day bonding and talking about all different sorts of subjects. We come from a very spiritual background and had some discussions of ghost and spirits earlier that day and into the evening. We were sitting outside at dusk when we heard a rustling in the leaves behind the out-building. The old lady next door likes to collect stray cats, and we thought it was most likely a cat finding its way back to her yard. Then we heard it again. This time it sounded like footsteps. I yelled "I'll call the police. You need to get out of my yard. " My daughter thought I was silly but went along anyway. We went into the home and locked all the windows and doors. I thought that maybe someone knew that my fellow was out of town, and we were home alone. That evening went on as a normal Sunday evening would.

My oldest daughter went to bed about 9:30 pm. My youngest daughter had just returned from weekend with her father. I went down in the basement to do some laundry. I came up the stairs with a load of laundry, and all my cabinets and drawers were wide open. They were so evenly opened you could have taken a ruler to measure, and I believe they would have been exact. At first I thought "Oh My God! Someone has broken into the home. " I yelled for my daughters, and they came running into the kitchen. A cold chill and goose bumps rose up on all of our skin. The kitchen became like ice, and we knew this was not a living person in the house. My youngest daughter has inherited an ability to speak with the other side. She kept hearing someone talking but was unable to make out what they were saying. She had previous experiences earlier in the month with what we felt was the same spirit. It was a girl or at least appeared as a girl. The energy this

130

spirit was carrying was of bad intent. You could feel it. We all felt it all around us.

I called a friend who was concerned that this could be someone that knew my boyfriend was out of town. She was worried that if we went to bed, they would show themselves. She insisted I call the police, so I did. The Grove City police department came to my home and searched the entire home. I even insisted they look into the attic. Nothing. They found nothing. I had locked all my doors and windows, and they had searched the home. No living human being in my home except my daughters and me. The following day my fellow came home. When he was in the home he was filled with anger and rage. This was not who he is. He is actually the farthest thing from these emotions. We would go out on the deck, and his anger would disappear. We would go into the home, and it would reappear. That day a good friend came over, and we cleansed the home.

I am lucky that throughout my travels I have encountered some unique people with some unique skills. I was aware of how to cleanse a home, but I felt I needed a little back-up. We cleansed, and as we were cleansing my cell phone would ring, and when I would answer no one was there. When I called the number that appeared on my phone, no one would answer. When I later talked with the person who owned this phone they denied ever calling. I have always felt when spirits are near.

I had never seen a ghost until this day. When cleansing the home a girl that appeared to be between twelve to sixteen walked down my driveway and turned and walked down the street. She was wearing blue jeans, a flannel shirt, and a hooded sweatshirt. Her sweatshirt hung in front of her face only revealing a small sliver of silvery blonde hair from beneath the hood of the sweatshirt. When cleansing I only asked that any spirits with bad intent were to leave our home. I later met a young woman that only lives a short distance from me. I overheard her telling a story about her

131

cabinets and drawers in her kitchen being opened just the same way mine were. I told her of my experience, and she then shared that she had seen this same girl in her front yard one stormy night. She said the girl had black eyes. My daughter had had a dream of this girl and thought maybe she had drowned in life. We looked to find a connection for this girl and our home, but to no avail. This girl also appeared on my daughter's television screen. She also tried to pull the blanket off of her while sleeping. The woman that shared this experience in her home went on to say that her mother was different. Her mother had been so angry and violent. That this was not her mother's normal way. I told the woman I met how to cleanse her home, and she has not had this experience since, and her mother is back to her old self.

Sometimes things are not what they appear to be. Beware or be aware!

Submitted by Jacqueline, Grove City, Ohio

. . . .

69.
Active Imaginations Or…

Rialto, California

I lived in Rialto in a single story house on Driftwood Avenue for about five years. I moved out in 2003. During the time I lived there with my teenage daughter and I experienced many strange happenings. The first incident was when the door from the garage to the house opened while I was trying to get my key. No one was inside the house to open the door. Of course I allowed my mind to create a logical reason for that happening. After that occurrence other things happened such as tapping on my bedroom window, toilets flushing, the sound of something extremely heavy falling (twice) in the area of the kitchen. However, nothing was out of place. My bedside lamps were sometimes flashing off and on, and they were plugged into different outlets. One lamp was plugged into a power strip that also serviced the alarm clock, which was not affected at all. Is this enough strangeness? Well, there is more, and keep in mind some of these things happened repeatedly while others only occurred once or twice.

There was unaccounted for music playing from the area of my daughter's room, but when I went to investigate the sound stopped. My daughter was not there - hhmm. My lab retriever, on a couple of occasions, sensed or saw something and became very protective of us while barking ferociously and starring at a certain spot in the garage. My doorbell would ring in the middle of the night, and no one was there. I have woken up in the night, and my TV was on. After the first time this happened I made sure my remote was on the dresser before I would go to sleep, so I know I did not roll over onto the remote. I felt someone/something brush my ankle as I walked. Dark shadows have also been seen in peripheral vision. One time there was a strange musty odor in a single spot in the hallway, suspended in the air about five feet from the floor.

These are only some of the things that took place in the 2400 block of Driftwood Avenue. At first I did not tell anyone. What would they think? Finally, I told a male friend - only because he reluctantly told me about some things he experienced there. He said he did not want me to be afraid, so he had been keeping it to himself, until he could no longer. While we were discussing this I tried to make light of it still by saying "maybe we both just have very active imaginations. " No sooner had I said this than the lamp between us came on. It was a touch lamp, and I probably would have found a way to justify that except it had not been plugged in for over a year because it was not working properly. It had a matching lamp, and I really liked the way they looked in the den, so we kept it for looks only. When we checked the lamp was plugged in. Who did it?

Fast forwarding two or three years after we moved from this house - which we loved dearly - my daughter and I were talking about paranormal stuff. It was a topic that they had discussed at school that day. She asked me if I believed in "that stuff. " (I had never mentioned anything to her about the experiences I had at the Rialto house because I did not want her to be afraid.) I told her that I do believe that unnatural things happen, and I have experienced some. She immediately began crying and asked me if it was at the Rialto house. It turned out that she had also experienced some things and did not want to say anything because she thought I would think she was nuts. I used to wonder why she never witnessed anything except the incident in the garage with the dog. I am curious to know if the people there now are experiencing anything strange.

Submitted by Regina, Rialto, California

. . . .

70.

They Were There First

Fort Irwin, California

I just recently moved from Fort Irwin. I lived on Pleiku Street. I had many activities in that house. I have seen a pioneer miner, a little girl, and moving objects. My son's bedroom door would lock itself when he was in the room, trapping him in that room. He never liked sleeping in his room until we got rosaries and crosses hanging over his bed. His closet door would open and close. It was a sliding door kind, even when we rigged it where it would not slide open, it still would. We propped his bedroom door open and left the lamps on. My daughter claimed that kids would play in her room or run into the toy room which is the big storage closet with the attic door. I hated that room since the attic door would be moved and open. Yes, I even put padlocks and hinges to keep it from moving, but they would be unlocked or pried apart. I would not let my kids play in that room. We would walk in grab a toy and barricade it.

When my fiancé would stay over the week he would see a little girl running from room to room. At first he thought it was my daughter, but he would see that she was in bed sleeping in her pajamas. This child was in a dress. The front door would be open even though we locked it. The screen door would still be locked. When I came home for lunch, I would feel tugging on my clothes, hear little footsteps running, and hearing children laughing, but I knew my kids were at school and at the sitter. One night we found an envelope with a child's baby teeth. The funny thing is it had been written in 2007. I had cleaned the house and moved in 2011. We later got some dogs, and they would growl at my son's room all the time or at the stairs. My house was never short of activities, footsteps, moving objects, or blinds literally flying off (it was hard to get them back on since it was a tight fit.) We have doors opening and closing, lights turning on and off, water faucets just running water, and children laughing and running (when mine were not home, or they were sleeping.) We also have things moving.

We just let it be. We even had a candle that exploded during the power outages (barely put a flame and they would explode.) My fiancé claims to have seen dark shadows and feel threatened by them as if telling him that he was unwelcome and to stay away from my family. I did not really feel threatened just upset when they messed with my kids. I know I attract the dark spirits. I always have. My children attract the white spirits. This sounds crazy I know, so if you move into that three-bedroom home, do not worry about the spirits, they were there first.

Submitted by LG, Fort Irwin, California

. . . .

71.
Do Not Provoke

Chesterfield, Virginia

I live in Chester and have always been skeptical of the paranormal. My cousin is a huge believer. To prove me wrong he made me mess with a Ouija board. Actually he made me mess with two different ones. Anyway two nights after that I started noticing strange things occur. Lights would flicker. Faucets were turned off, and my door would open. I have heard heavy banging and loud growls. The strangest thing was the front side and back doors would always open. Of course I told my friends and family, even my girlfriend, and they all thought I was going crazy or was just too tired to realize that it was my imagination. I was thinking the same thing, but why not tell somebody?

One night I was sitting on my bed. I got up and came back with a drink. I was half way in my room when I heard a growl. I shrugged it going "this isn't anything new. Who cares?" I sat on my bed. Dead silence. Then I heard a growl like a bull when they sigh. At the same time my shirt fluttered. There was no current since I blocked my heater, and I have covered my windows with blankets, (I have this fear I'll look through a window at night and see a face other than mine) so there is no explanation. I soon went to bed and woke up the next morning. The whole day I thought about it. I came home and said "look. I don't know who you think you are, but you're not scaring me. Show yourself you coward!" I have fears but I am not scared of things that go bump in the night. I provoked it even when my cousin said not to. Oh well I was not scared, so I provoked. I started shouting "Come on. All you've got is a couple bangs and growls ha! My cat makes scarier noises!"

After fifteen minutes of this I decided to stop. I was not getting much, so why continue? Well, I walked in my room and flicked the lights on since my windows are covered. It was always pitch black in there. I was about to sit on my bed when I felt a presence.

137

My hair stood up, and I got goose bumps. I turned around, and I saw a 6-foot-2 black shadow. It had no features. It was just a black shadow. Arms were long, and legs were long with its heard cocked to the side. I said with a scared voice "you don't scare me. " Truth was it did, but at the same time it was a rush of excitement. I tried to touch it, but my hand just went straight through it. Then it disappeared. I went to take a shower, and I noticed three scratches on my back. I still provoke it, but it has not shown itself since. I just hear noises and growls. I am thinking about filming it. Maybe be a ghost hunter because that was awesome. I loved it. I am a believer now.

Submitted by Damon, Chesterfield, Virginia

. . . .

72.
Evil Aunt

Noblesville, Indiana

I have an aunt that I was told practiced witchcraft. She out of the blue sent a package to my house, and I opened it. When I opened the package I realized that it was meant for my niece that just had a baby because it had a baby outfit in it that she purchased. I gave it to my niece. As soon as I opened the package weird things started happening in my house. My son and my husband would be sick quite a bit. We would see a black image in our hallway. The dog would be looking at something barking, and there would not be anything there. He would stand outside the kitchen and bark and would not go in. My son had his room and bathroom in the basement. He was standing down there and felt a burning on his back. He had me look at his back, and he had scratches across his back. Several times my son's television would turn on by itself. One time my son was coming out of his bathroom, and a friend said he saw a black shadow behind him. Our doorbell would ring, and there would be nobody there. This happened on many occasions waking us up at night.

I feel like someone is standing over me at night. One night I tried to rise up, and something was holding me to the bed. I woke up, and my right shoulder and arm were bruised. I woke up and had bruises on my arms and legs. I did not know how I got them. I have also heard someone say "mom" a few times, but my son was not around. My niece also started having things happen in her house (she no longer lives there.) She would put some things on her counter and turn around, and they were moved. She had things fly across her kitchen on several occasions. She was on the computer doing homework with someone, and they had the webcam on talking to each other. The person on the other end asked her who just walked behind her. Nobody else was there. The lights then went out in the house. Her baby was also sick a lot before she moved out of the house.

Right after the package arrived at my house my sister just happened to have gone to a psychic. She told her that our aunt was practicing witchcraft because things were going on with her and the family. The psychic said to get rid of the package and clothing that she sent. She said my aunt put a spell on it wanting to harm someone, either myself or her daughter or the baby. I then went to see the psychic and took with me a picture of my mom and her 4 siblings. The psychic looked at the picture and pointed to my aunt and said that she was the evil one. I am not really sure what is going on, but it has me spooked. It is just all too weird.

Submitted by Spooked, Noblesville, Indiana

. . . .

73.

A House on Windy Hill Court
Wofford Heights, California

My experience began when I moved into a house on Windy Hill Court in Wofford Heights, CA in 2012. I was eight months pregnant with my youngest child. When I walked into the house for the first time, I could feel there was something wrong, but I just ignored it. The first night we had no lights, and we (my husband and I and my two children at the time) had to sleep in the living room. The lights were getting turned on the next day. All my children and my husband were asleep, and I was half asleep when I heard a woman scream. It was as if she was in pain, but I ignored it thinking it was one of the neighbors, and I fell back to sleep. The next morning I told my husband about it, and that was when he told me about the two people who had died in the house. Nobody knows how they died. He said he did not want to scare me because I can see, smell, and talk to spirits, and I was trying to get away from them.

Everything was quiet for a little bit after that night until we moved into our front bedroom. That was when everything went bad. I started not wanting to sleep. I could not sleep when I was in the bedroom. One night my husband was in the living room watching TV, and I was in the room trying to sleep, I had a feeling somebody was in the room with me. I sat up in bed, and there was an old lady at the foot of the bed. I could not talk or move for what seemed like hours. I turned and looked towards the door wanting to scream for my husband and the door slammed shut. The old lady moved closer to me walking through my bed, and that was when my husband came in to ask me why I slammed the door. I jumped out of bed and grabbed him. He asked me why I was shaking so badly. I told him what had happened. He said he believed me, but I could see in his eyes that he did not.

Some time went by without any incidents. One day when it was raining our ceiling started to leak, so my husband went into our attic to fix the leak. He fixed the leak, and when he came down he was white as a ghost. He told me he believed me about the house being haunted. I asked him what he had seen, and he would not tell me. He said that it would scare me so badly. A lot of things have been happening that are unexplainable. Those are just a few of the experiences that have happened here. There are tons more. I am mainly sharing my story with y'all in the hopes of getting help with these spirits. I still live in the house to this day.

Submitted by Dana, Wofford Heights, California

. . . .

74.
It Would Not Leave

Fort Drum, New York

We just moved because of how bad things were getting. It got so bad I called a priest to bless my house. I also got a hold of paranormal investigators, but it got so bad after the priest came I did not want I upset it anymore. This took place on Forsythe Loop. I am writing this in case the next people happen to have things happen and see this. We moved to our apartment in February 2013. I was pregnant when we moved there, but we had a dog. My husband would be gone a lot for training. My dog would stare for a long time at the hallway or bathroom and blank walls. Sometimes she would bark. I thought it was strange but ignored it. My husband noticed it as well. We knew out dog was being bothered by something.

We brought our baby home in May. Things got worse once she came home. Things would go missing (mostly baby items.) Doors would slam. We would hear a baby cry, but nothing would be there. One night we put our child in our room to sleep. We closed the door, and it would immediately open. You had to literally twist the handle and push the door to open it. The fact that it was going near our baby freaked us out. We spent the night in a hotel, then with friends. We went back and pretended nothing happened. My husband talked to his mother about what was going on, and she talked to her medium. She said that something bad happened there. She said that it was a small child. She then told us to look into the criminal records. I went to the MPS and talked to someone who completely believed me. Sadly they did not have records going more then a few years back. The woman told us we should move. She said "this is more common than you think. "

We talked about moving. We decided to wait it out. I seriously wish we did not. My husband was working overnight, and I just put the baby to sleep. I was getting into bed when I saw

143

something white walk by the room. The energy changed. We left with just the clothes on our back. We saw a priest. He felt the energy but assured me whatever it was it would leave. As a strict Catholic I believed that by the power of Jesus Christ this thing would leave. It did not. My husband even saw a little boy in 1990s clothing. We left in November 2013. I am so thankful we did. I will not even drive by the house. I pray whatever it was it does not scare others.

Submitted by Kelly, Fort Drum, New York

. . . .

75.

Smelly Lady

Portland, Texas

I lived on Pecos St. in Portland two years ago after my father got a job at Kiwiett and I occasionally went to the park at night to jog by Frio Dr. On two different occasions I saw a lady on the corner fence beside the park just staring at me. I ran by her the first time and there was an overwhelming horrible smell of fish or dead animal coming from where she was. I saw her head moving and following me in every direction. I would jog around the park, so the second time I ran by her I decided to be nice and say hello.

Just as I was getting close to her again I got hit by the horrible smell but I smiled at her and said "hi", she actually said something back but I couldn't make out what it was. She had a long grayish skirt with a blouse tucked into it and her hair was in a side pony tail.

I didn't make a big deal out of it but a week later I saw her again on the same spot and wearing the same thing. I arrived at the park before she did and honestly I never noticed where she had come from. She was just there when I turned around. I was jogging back home and I knew I had to jog by her again. This time I got nervous because there wasn't anyone at the park. As I got closer to her she just kept staring at me. And as soon as I was right by her she said please help me and actually grabbed my wrist.. I got freaked out so bad I don't even remember how I got home, I just ran as fast as I could. I was afraid that if I stopped she would be right behind me.

When I got home my dad was having a late night snack and he said to me "Teresa, gosh you smell like a dead sardine, you're making me lose my appetite! " that was the same smell that lady had.. I told my dad what had happened and he wanted to call the authorities because he said it could've been an assault but I refused because I had a feeling she wasn't even human, her hand felt cold and wet.

Does anyone know about someone dying in water here in Portland? I moved in with my mom in another area of Portland because I can't even drive by that park at night. PLEASE PLEASE BELIEVE ME AND DON'T BE THERE AT NIGHT ON YOUR OWN.

Submitted by Anonymous, Portland, Texas

. . . .

146

76.
Creepy Apartment

Goleta, California

When I went to UCSB I stayed in S.C.E. Village, which was an apartment complex for transfers and graduate students. The building was brand new when I moved there in 2008. However, the land completely surrounding it was developed and used a few decades prior.

After a couple months of living there people started to notice weird things happening. There would be dripping sounds in the gutters even though it had not rained. Roommates began to argue with one another (nothing new). Also, some girls would feel something cold holding them down when they were sleeping.

One night while I was in bed I woke up in a panic. There, right in front of me, was a girl with her back towards me. My door was locked, and I did not let anyone in prior. She was staring into my closet, swaying, with long dark hair. Like the sissy I am, I closed my eyes and ran to the light. When I flipped it on, she was gone.

Fast forward a month later. My friend had a girl in his room. They heard something run in his closet and shut the door. Thinking it was his roommate, my buddy turned the light on, yelled, and opened the closet. It was empty. The girl got so scared she left. Later that same week our neighbor was in the laundry room, which was directly below my friend's bedroom. She felt a presence in there with her, so she took a picture of the corner (which of course was on my old phone), and when put on negative mode a face can be seen in one of the dryers. A girl's face.

It is Celtic tradition to burn blue candles to ward off spirits. I did this, and the tips burned red.

I do not know what it is we all saw and felt, but it seemed to have some hostility toward girls, and a curiosity with guys. Something about the building did not seem right to anyone. It was creepy, and the architecture felt like a prison and cast weird shadows. There was some reason it remained undeveloped for so long. I do not know what it was, just glad I do not live there anymore.

Submitted by Brandon, Goleta, California

. . . .

77.

Man With The White Pants

Greenwich, Ohio

Back in 1983, I rode my bike to my "then" girlfriend's mother's home to hang out on Halloween, to watch the movie Halloween. On my way through town I noticed an older man (50-60 years old) with slender build. He was probably six feet tall walking the sidewalk downtown. Small town and all, I had never seen the man before. I noticed he was wearing white pants and a dark blue or black windbreaker which I found peculiar I do not know why, it was October I guess. He just seemed out of place. Not so much the windbreaker, but those white pants. They looked very clean, like brand new. I continued to my girlfriend's just past the laundry mat.

We ate munchies and watched Halloween. It was getting late and time for me to head home. I had parked my bike out back by their back steps, so I had to walk through the dining room and kitchen to get to the back door. When I got into the kitchen I looked outside the back door glass, and the man in the white pants was staring dead at me! I turned to get my girlfriend and her mother's attention to tell them what I was seeing.

When I looked again, he was gone. We looked out other windows down the driveway and out front of the house, but he had simply vanished! I was freaked out. Normally things do not scare me much, but this was different because I had seen this guy earlier that evening downtown walking. Once we had turned on the back lights, I jumped on my bike, and burned rubber!

My mother and sister had been visiting out of town, and I was home alone. I camped out on the living room couch. When my mother got home she woke me up asking me what I was doing sleeping with her butcher knife. I never saw the man in white

149

pants ever again, but when I saw him standing behind the girlfriend's house peering at me, it freaked me out, and still does today.

Submitted by Edinger, Greenwich, Ohio

. . . .

78.

My Great Grandmother

Houlton, Maine

My grandmother's house is an 1850s farm house (give or take a few years) off Ludlow Road on Callaghan, and we have always felt odd things. There used to be a trailer in the same driveway that my parents lived in when I was a baby. One morning at about 4:00 am my father was on his way out for work, and he looked up at my grandparents' house and saw what appeared to be my grandmother waving to him from the window. Later that day he told my mother he saw her mom, and she asked where. He described where, and my mother's response was "My parents are away, and that's the sealed off attic. " My father is a strong skeptic of ghosts or anything paranormal or cryptic, but he still tells that story.

The house has a nook off the living room where there is a bed for guests, and you can clearly see the TV and living room from the bed. There is also a desk with a computer in the room. One afternoon I was lying on the bed, and my grandmother came in and grabbed something off the bed and went back out to the kitchen. A few minutes later I looked over to the coffee table and saw her staring down at it. It looked like her reading a newspaper that was lying on the table. I turned around and thought nothing of it. Later I went to the kitchen and asked her what she was reading. My grandmother told me she had not been back into the room since she got whatever it was off the desk. I feel like my dad and I have seen the same woman, and my mother said the way we describe her sounded like it was her grandmother. There have been numerous deaths in the house, (all old age and illness, nothing to note) but my great-grandmother actually died in the trailer (which has since been moved). Mom said she could sense male spirits in the house.

Submitted by Brandon, Houlton, Maine

79

A Few Scary Experiences

Martinez, California

My ex and I lived on Foster Street. Little did I know how close to the cemetery we were because I may have reconsidered moving there. It was a spacious two-bedroom apartment with a window overlooking the marina, but something about that room creeped me out. I never liked being in there alone. My newborn daughter hated being in there as well. It never got any sunlight because of where the wall was facing. The sun did not hit it. I always had to close the closet door when I was in there which was a small walk-in closet. I did not like it open.

Twice I saw things. One time I was walking to my daughter's room. As I walked past my room, I saw something out of the corner of my eye that was white, bright, and tall as a human. It was rushing straight to my closet door. I froze where I was and had to yell for my ex to come over. I was scared to death. Another time I was in my daughter's room, turned around, and saw what I thought looked like a teenager guy.

He was probably between fifteen or sixteen. He dressed like he was from the 1990s. He disappeared. Another time I was sitting on the couch in my living room, and where I was I could see down the hall to my child's bedroom. There she was, standing in her crib, talking and reaching out to someone who was not there, as if they were going to pick her up.

I hated living there. It was an inconvenience with the steep hill, and there was just something about it that I could not shake. I never liked being home alone with my kid; we always left to make sure we were not. In all honesty, the crack heads downstairs were probably the scariest thing. We only lived there for about a year and a half. Some people feel attached to homes where they first bring their babies home. I sure was not attached. Definitely a few scary experiences.

Submitted by JP, Martinez, California

. . . .

80.
A Picket Fence Smile

Riverside, California

This happened in 1978 between July and September on Stobbs Street Riverside, California. I do not know the address but was told that it happened in some apartments. My parents were sleeping one night when suddenly my father woke up and started hitting my mother then jumped out of bed then ran down stairs where she found him staring at the wall. My father said he was asleep then felt something tickling his feet. He thought it was my mother. He opened his eyes and saw something in bed in between them. He started punching at it but was unable to hit it. Whatever it was jumped out of bed and ran downstairs where he continued to fight with it. It then ran into the wall after knocking down a small statue "which turned to dust" leaving a perfect off colored circle into the paint. My mother had come downstairs only to see him with scratches looking at the wall.

A couple of days later, my mother had just put me to sleep when she saw something down the downstairs hallway smiling at her. At that moment my dad walked through the door from work scaring her. My mom turned to my dad telling him "that wasn't funny. " She then looked down the hall only to see that nothing was there. The description of this thing only varies by height. When my dad was fighting it, it was around four feet tall. When my mother saw it, it seemed like it was taller or was floating. Both claimed that it was wearing an Arabian/Sheik outfit with a headdress. They said that its skin was pinkish with three fingers or talons. Its eyes were large, black, and sunken. My mom described the smile as a picket fence. It was at this same place that my older brother had seen a shadow figure on the door with glowing eyes which caused him to have an asthma attack.

Submitted by Dale, Riverside, California

. . . .

154

81.

Dark Cloud

Westville, Oklahoma

I am still unsure what I saw near the old Corntassel Cemetery southwest of Westville. This cemetery was an early Cherokee family cemetery started, I think, shortly after the Trail of Tears. I was going south from US Hwy 62 onto Ross Swimmer Road South to go pick up a friend, so we could go to a football game (fall of 2013.) When I got down into the old Addielee Community and his house, we left and came back on the same road. We got right to the Corntassel Cemetery, and we both saw a dark small wispy cloud leave the graveyard, cross in front of my pickup and on into the thick deep forest.

I had never seen a dark cloud like that ever. It never did evaporate or separate! It stayed in one cloud form. It never did make a shape of any kind. It just curled and flowed like smoke or a small cloud but dark gray or charcoal colored. We stopped the pick-up right there by the cemetery and looked at each other. What was it? It was like nothing I had ever seen. If it was a ghost, it was not white, and it never formed into a human shape. Was it a spirit of something? Was it a demon from hell? We cannot say for sure. We both have traveled this road many times since that evening, but it never happened again. So far!

When I was growing up here I would hear stories from the elders in my family about the Cherokee communities around Westville, especially the old Addielee area and the woods behind Christie. This cemetery is in that general area. My granddad told me he was a kid when he heard stories about the old Addielee Witch back around the turn of the 20th century (1900.) It gives one the creeps to think there are still unexplainable things out there that we still encounter!

Submitted by Rocky, Westville, Oklahoma

82.
Man In A Black Suit

Magnolia, Texas

I purchased property in Inverness Crossing in Magnolia, TX in 2001. I cleared it and had a new doublewide home placed there. After moving in my boys started saying there was a ghost in the house and I laughed it off ...

Until ... One day I was home alone washing dishes when I heard a noise and turned to look. There was a man dressed in a black suit with a black hat on standing at the far side of the living room. Then he was gone! It made my heart go pitter-pat.

There was no one in the house but me and I was creeped out! We would hear strange noises and stuff. I finally said aloud "If you want to stay then you must be quiet and remain hidden when I, my family, or guests are here."

After that when I came home and walked up to an empty house I could hear what sounded like someone running inside. Since that time there are very few incidents that occur in that home. I also have a building out back with a loft and my son lived our there for a while.

He would say creepy things happened. One day his girlfriend was there alone and a pot sitting on the counter flew across the room at her. She ran crying out of there and would not go back in until he got back home.

I think the ghost did not like her because it has never done anything mean before or since. We have also seen a shadowy figure of a man in black on the roof on the property before. I think the property is haunted because there were no existing buildings there when I bought it.

I don't mind as long as we exist there in harmony together. Who knows maybe someday I will need his help.

Submitted by Ginger, Magnolia, Texas

83.
Our Little Guest

Buckeye, Arizona

I was also born and raised in this little town, and I cannot even tell you how often these types of events happen. Buckeye has to be one of the most haunted places around. When I was growing up my little brother, my mom, and I lived in an apartment complex, and I can still remember all of the crazy things that went on in our apartment. Lights would be turning on and off on their own; the toilet would flush on its own. The faucet would turn on and off. And sometimes If our little guest would become upset, there would be loud crashes coming from our kitchen. It would sound like everything from the cupboards was thrown to the floor at the same time. When we would get to the kitchen to see what happened though, everything was in its right place except for all the cupboard doors and drawers would be open.

At one point my mom was accused of changing the locks on our apartment because apparently the manager at the time was trying to get into our apartment, but her key would not open the door. When my mom questioned the manager's reason for needing to get in without my mom there, the manager stammered a bit before saying that it was an emergency, and she could not get in. However, when she used her key in front of my mom, it worked just fine. I am guessing she lied about the 'emergency' and our guest did not like her one bit. We lived in that apartment for a couple of years, and the day that we were packing to move out, there was a very sad, sad melody being played on what sounded like a harmonica. It seemed to be right in the room with us yet, no one else could hear it.

Submitted by Kristi, Buckeye, Arizona

. . . .

84.

A Haunted House

Coos Bay, Oregon

A few years back a lot of my friends and I were building the haunted house in the Little Theatre on the Bay that we did every year. The person in charge of haunted house gave us permission to stay the night to work on the set and just for our own amusement. We knew LTOB was haunted. There are two stories and three entities that were seen there that I know of. One is of a young lady who while in the ladies room had fallen off the ledge into one of the stalls. She hit her head on the sink counter and died. The other two are a young boy and girl but I do not know their story of why they are there.

The night we stayed in LTOB we did some work and then when it got late we decided to break out a Ouija board to see if we could contact the spirits. Our first try we believe we had contacted the young lady. She was very nice and there wasn't anything too interesting that happened talking to her. We told her good bye and then tried again. We got the little girl. She told us her brother was there with her and they liked to play. Upstairs we had a room for the haunted house that was full of doors that led nowhere. The exit door would slam when you went through it. Well we asked them to let us know they were there, and directly after we asked that the exit door upstairs on the stage slammed. Everyone was downstairs with us either participating or watching. It was the creepiest thing I have ever experienced even though all of spirits that stayed there were supposedly nice and liked to play.

Submitted by Samantha, Coos Bay, Oregon
. . . .

85.
A Wet Dog

Fort Worth, Texas

This happened in 1970. We lived in this big old house that once was a mansion. It had three floors to it. Actually I think the third floor must have been the attic now that I think about it. That was where we lived. It was on Hemphill Street close to Morningside. The house is no longer there. Anyway, to get to our apartment on the top floor you had to enter the door on the second floor. Our three kids were in New Mexico with my parents. My husband got up to go to work that morning, and everything was normal. Then it got weird.

I must have dozed off. I heard the keys in the door on the second floor and heard footsteps coming up the stairs. I called out "did you forget something?" Well, nothing was there, and I thought it was my imagination. I went back to sleep. Then I heard this noise out on Hemphill like a car crash. I got up, looked out, and yep car crash, then I went back to sleep. Well, I did not know if I really got out of bed or not. The one window in our bedroom was floor level, and someone could fall out of it, so I could see out that window pretty well. I went back to sleep.

I remember seeing a wet dog now when the car crash happened. It was raining but not in reality. Somehow a wet dog had got in to my apartment. Ok, it was not threatening or anything, and I just could not stay awake. When I did finally wake up I remembered all that had transpired. I thought "Whoa! What a wild dream!" BUT when my feet hit the floor there was a puddle of water right where the dog had sat. Spooky to say the least.

Submitted by Glitz, Fort Worth, Texas
. . . .

86.

Old Orphanage

Mantorville, Minnesota

I grew up in an old house in Mantorville, built in 1863. I was thirteen years old when we moved in, and immediately things started happening. The bedspread would be pulled up while I was sleeping. Doors would slam shut. I could hear someone walking around upstairs at night, and the old doors would rattle when they would walk up to them.

I also would hear kids giggling and playing. They would play with my three-year-old sister's toys. In the middle of the night I would hear my little sister telling them to leave her alone. She said she just wanted to sleep. Throughout my teenage years I would come home around 2:00 or 3:00 am from babysitting or hanging with my friends. I would pull in the drive way and sit watching the house for a little bit. All the lights would be out, but I could see the glow from the clock on the microwave. I could see someone walking back and forth in front of the microwave clock. I also would see a shadow of someone standing in the window watching.

For the first couple of years I lived in this house I was completely freaked out by all of this and more. After I finally got my parents to recognize something was going on, we did a little research and found that the house had been an orphanage for children during the flu epidemic in the early 1900s. This completely explained the children. There are also some adults in the house. I am not exactly sure where they came from. However, after twenty years the house has settled down a lot, and my parents love living there!

Submitted by Shawny, Mantorville, Minnesota

. . . .

87.
Tall Black Figure

Brownsville, Texas

Ever since I was about 12 I have been able to hear a woman's voice calling my name at random times of the day at my moms house. Never once have I been harmed by what I know I am surrounded by. I have even heard the giggles of a little girl. I have heard knocking, have experienced the light going on and off. My TV turning on and footsteps in the hall when no one was home.

One night around February 2012 at 2:45 am I went to lay on my bed ready to turn in for the night. As I closed my eyes within 20 minutes of me sleeping I felt someone next to me staring at me. But I could not open my eyes, I could hear my husband snoring but I was unable to move.

I began to feel a pressure on my chest and I was unable to breathe. I caught myself gasping for air. I was able to move my head side to side and when I was finally able to open my eyes there was a tall black figure. I could tell it was a man, I could see the pants and the overcoat, and it felt so angry.

As I looked at him I still could not breathe. Within seconds I was able to sit up, and being rendered motionless neck down I then awoke my husband scared and gasping for air. He rushed me out of the room into the living room but I could still feel the presence lingering. I was unable to go back into my room for about 30 minutes.

I have experienced many physical encounters but never one so aggressive, and of all those times this was one of the few that frightened me.

Submitted by Windy, Brownsville, Texas

. . . .

88.

13 Bends

Buena Vista, Pennsylvania

In the summer of 1966 my friend Louie (R.I.P.) and I spent the day drinking beer at a place along the Mon River near 13 Bends. Louie suggested we spend the night at 13 Bends in order to prove it was not haunted. We drove down the winding road across the tracks to the cemetery and went to sleep in his long black 58 Cadillac limousine. I was asleep in the back seat, Louie in the front when we were awakened by a tapping on the driver' side front window. There was the face of a grizzled old man. It was light out, and with the help of all the beer we had drunk the night before we had slept through the night. The man then suggested that we pull the car over in the shade because it being black it would soon heat up like an oven. We had slept undisturbed by any supernatural creatures of any kind.

I recently related this story to another old friend. He had his own 13 Bends' story much different than mine. He and some others in the same time frame were parked near the tracks one night when they saw a light swinging from side to side coming up the tracks towards them. The closer it came, the more worried they became. They went to leave only to find their car stuck. They had to get out and push it free. They then took off in a panic before the swinging light and whomever was wielding it reached them. It could have been a ghost or just someone out walking the tracks late at night. Only God knows the answer.

Submitted by Cliff, Buena Vista, Pennsylvania

. . . .

89.

On Maple Valley Hwy

Maple Valley, Washington

I do not usually like talking about things like this because I think it is ridiculous; however, my experience was quite a trip. It started back in November 2013 on Maple Valley Hwy in between Renton and Maple Valley right before the river where the guardrail runs along for a half a mile or so. I passed through a thick patch of fog briefly and saw a black figure pass along in front of me. The cars driving toward me had flashed lights and halted as if they saw what I saw. It was not a person and disappeared. It looked like a shadow. I did not really think too much into it, even though it startled me a little bit.

Now fast forward to February 26th, 2014 driving around the same time and the same area. Similar thing had happened. I completely forgot about last November and was on my way home. I was driving home along Maple Valley Hwy around 9:30 pm passing the guardrail, and a figure jumped in front of my car running from right to left. It was tall, skinny, and black. It was passing quickly. As my eyes followed it, a bird possibly a hawk or a bat came flying to my windshield making it hard to see. It was just staying right in front of me. After about ten seconds it flew away. I have never been so afraid, and THANK GOD I did not panic and crash my car. I am trying to think of ALL logical explanations for this. Next time I will just take Hwy 18 home. I promise I am not crazy!

Submitted by A.S.FromRenton, Maple Valley, Washington

. . . .

90.

Gas Station Attendant

Greensboro, North Carolina

I lived on the corner of High Point Road and Alamance Road across the former Jefferson Pilot Property. I used to see a man dressed like a gas station attendant from the 1940s, with a grey overall and black hair (I must have seen him a total of seven times from 1991-1992.) It looked as if he were to walk from my room (which was directly on the street side) towards HP road (towards the street.) He walked as if he was on a mission to get somewhere. He never made eye contact with me. He never did anything evil. I got used to it. After three times seeing this, it did not scare me anymore.

The problem is that during the time I lived there, an accident happened directly on High Point Road right in front of my house claiming the life of three innocent people in different cars. I was eating dinner when the police came to ask for a PHONE! (I guess cell phones were not popular then.) In any case I could not bring myself to tell the police that perhaps they had seen a ghost and gotten scared. This was in October or November of 1992. I moved in 1993. The painter who was prepping the house told me to find some other painter, because he kept seeing a grey shadow inside my house, and he was scared! I wonder if the current residents of that house have noticed anything unusual there. In those days we did not have twitter, or YouTube. We could have posted there for evidence.

Submitted by Sara, Greensboro, North Carolina

. . . .

91.
Josh

Riverton, Wyoming

I lived in the Wind River Estates for about a year. Nothing out of the ordinary had happened until I got pregnant with my son. We had little things like objects going missing then showing up randomly in a strange location in the house. This began when I was about four months pregnant. I would hear footsteps in my kitchen and scratching in my walls. It got to the point where I did not like to be alone in that house. My two-year-old daughter started telling me about a little boy named Josh that she played with in the house all of the time.

Strange thing is that we had never said that name to her. She would run screaming from her bedroom, "mommy Josh scared me!" One time she woke up at 3:00 am and flooded the house by clogging the sink and letting the water run. Then she went back to bed and said that Josh told her to. This was getting way too creepy for me! I was told by the previous owners that their daughter-in-law had died in my bedroom, but that did not explain "Josh. " One night my fiancé and I were in the bedroom, and a box flew off of my closet shelf at us. Another time when we were in the bedroom again three candles flew off of our dresser at us. Again being on the bed, the fan came off of the night stand and knocked my fiancé in the head! It was not more than four months after I gave birth to our son that we packed up and moved.

Submitted by AJ, Riverton, Wyoming
. . . .

92.
Don't Know What's Going On.

Los Banos, California

My family home is not old. We live in Ranchwood. We were the first and only people who have lived in our house. Going on twenty-three years now, but I remember as a teenager strange things happening. We lived in a two-story house and would hear someone running in the hallway upstairs. Even though there was no one up there. In the kitchen my sister and I were talking when it sounded like nails scratching on the floor next to us. It was like something trying to run fast, but when we looked down we only heard it. We did not see it. As we got older the activity seemed to stop.

I still live in the house with my son and other family members. The activity started up again, only more intense. I remember being upstairs on the computer, and I kept hearing my young niece calling my name. I asked her what she wanted, but she just kept calling my name, so I went to see what she wanted. I looked down the stairs at her and saw that she just ran off. Thinking she was playing with me because I just saw her run off, I went to find her. She was nowhere to be found. Come to find out she was not even home. She left to the store with her Mom. I was home all by myself.

I could write on forever; so many things have happened and are still happening. I will not write down the really scary stuff that has happened here, and I cannot explain what is going on here.

Submitted by Natalie, Los Banos, California

. . . .

93.

Not sure What It Was

Farmington, New Mexico

When I was sixteen years old (I am fifty-three now) my dad and I went deer hunting at Mistinas Peak in the Carson National Forest. We walked about half a mile as the sun was just coming up. We sat on the edge of a canyon overlooking a big area that had a deep wash down the bottom. We spotted something far down in the wash. It was walking on two legs, and it looked like a man with a fur suit on that covered him from head to toe. My dad saw it first. My dad was never scared when we were in the woods hunting. It seemed strange that a man would be walking during HUNTING season with a fur coat on when you are supposed to be dressed in blaze orange.

My dad said "What the hell is that in the canyon?" He was looking through his binoculars. I pulled my rifle up that had a four-power scope and sighted in on what he was pointing at. I saw a large human type-thing walking up the wash for about five to ten seconds. It was NOT a man. It was the closest thing to a Sasquatch that I had ever seen. We could not tell exactly what it was. We thought if it was a man in a fur suit during hunting season, he was crazy, and we did not need to be near him. We left the area we were hunting, got in the pickup, and drove twenty miles away. To this day I think that it could have been a sasquatch or a big foot.

Submitted by Larry, Farmington, New Mexico

. . . .

94.
The Man With The Top Hat
Castalia, North Carolina

I rented this little house walking distance from Taylor's store. Before I moved in there was a lot of work that had to be done. One of the first things I noticed were crosses in olive oil over the doorways in the home. We painted the entire house, and those crosses never disappeared. At the time my boys were three and five. My oldest son would never stay in that house for some reason. He always wanted to stay with my mom.

Well, one night he stayed, and he woke me up early the next morning crying to leave and go to my mom's house. He told me he saw a man in the kitchen with a top hat on. A couple of months went by, and one night we were watching horror movies with all the lights off. This was summer time, so we had a fan going to help cool it off. Once the movie went off before anyone could turn on the light we heard this loud thump. We turned on the light to find the fan lying in the other room in the middle of the floor. No one touched it, so how did it get there was the question.

Well, I moved maybe two months after that. Almost four years after I moved one of my friends showed me a picture that had been taken inside the home. Sitting there on the left hand corner was a face of the man with the top hat.

Submitted by Kandice, Castalia, North Carolina
. . . .

95.

Mr. B

Holley, New York

We lived in a house on West Albion Street in Holley, New York in the 1980s. It was a large Victorian with two staircases and five bedrooms. In the front foyer there was a lovely staircase with a "B" on the post and a stained glass window with fish half way up the stairs. At the top of the stairs there was a door we kept closed during the cold weather. Often times our cage of parakeets downstairs would be screeching and making all kinds of noises in the middle of the night. Footsteps could be heard coming up the stairs, and then the door would be opened.

I often times covered my head with a sheet, so that I did not have to see what was coming up the stairs. At the bottom of the stairs my husband kept his desk. After of a night of birds screeching, footsteps, and doors opening, items on my husband's desk would be moved. We called the ghost Mr. B. After selling the house, we were told the next occupants actually saw Mr. B. in the master bedroom and the living room. Who knows? I always hid and never saw Mr. B. I do not think he ever harmed anyone. He was just hang around and let us know he was there.

Submitted by Kate, Holley, New York

. . . .

96.
Brenda And Her Mamaw

Cohutta, Georgia

I moved into our home on Cleveland Hwy in Cohutta about two years ago. Since moving in we have heard a little girl laughing and have seen shadows of a person and a child as well. My three-year-old said her friend Brenda lived in her brother's closet. She said Brenda lived here with us, and this is Brenda's Mamaw's house. I asked what Brenda looked like, she said as tall as my 11-year-old daughter. Brenda has yellow hair, and she wears a pretty pink dress, and her Mamaw is big and has short hair.

Lights would go on and off, and we heard a girl say "Mommy" when it was just my aunt and I here. I did not think and replied "what?" Then my aunt reminded me that we were alone. It gave us cold chills. My husband who is a non believer now says he cannot explain what we hear, but it is something. We still hear toys and dolls going off and see shadows daily. I just pay it no mind.

Submitted by Ashley, Cohutta, Georgia

. . . .

97.

Apalachee Heritage

Dacula, Georgia

We purchased a house in Apalachee Heritage in Dacula, Georgia. We moved in at the end of October in 2011. It is a beautiful home and a quiet subdivision. Having moved to Georgia from Iowa I rarely thought about ghosts or history of the land. My other half works from home. I cannot even tell you when things began to get ugly, but I moved out in April of 2013, when he was out of town visiting family, without his knowledge. I felt great terror of him by the time of my escape. A friend of mine took some pictures of our dogs playing together while I was packing and moving. A few days later she sent them to me and told me to look closely at them. Out of about ten pictures, four of them had orbs. One of the orbs was super scary looking. It had swirls throughout. I still get goose bumps when I look at it.

My other half and I met in Iowa, dated, and lived together for about a year and a half prior to moving to Georgia. We rented a house in Buford and lived there for the first year and a half prior to buying and moving into the home we purchased in Dacula. I was so excited. It was everything I thought I would never be able to afford in Iowa. You get so much more home for your money here compared to Iowa! Little did I know this would become a house full of anger, crying, and fighting constantly.

The first thing I remember that seemed out of character for my other half was strange. I remember we had recently moved in, and I was out in the garage smoking. I did not smoke in the house, but it was chilly outside. He had come out to join me and noticed I was wearing my slippers. He jumped on me about wearing them back inside after being in the garage with them on. First of all this was my house too and how dare he speak to me like I was his child and not his partner. Second of all, the garage floor was very clean, and it was not the big deal that he made it out to be. I do not

171

remember if I said anything to him about it but tucked it away in my memories.

Slowly but surely all of that kind of behavior escalated from my partner. I would be crying hysterically in a corner somewhere in the house. It seemed I could not get him to stop until I screamed at him. Before long I was yelling bad things to him about himself as well. One can only endure so much. I would hate myself for yelling. It was not who I was. I hated fighting. There was no reason to ever fight when you are a mature adult and your children do not live with you and have their own lives and family. These are supposed to be the calm and happy years of the empty nesters.

I got to a point that I felt as though I was on pins and needles in my own home. Being that he was working from home, I was rarely home alone. I worked on the weekends outside of the home doing sales. Monday through Thursday I would clean the big house that never seemed to be dust free and take the dogs to the nearby dog park daily. My golden retriever and golden mix became my sanity. I do not know how I would have made it without them. I found myself and my life spinning out of control becoming depressed and suicidal while my partner seemed to turn into a very angry person. Someone I no longer knew. I would take long baths or just lie in bed crying. My golden would always stay by my side and give me a reason to snap out of it. The arguing was a daily thing that would last up to hours of going round and round about the same stuff over and over again.

I was made to feel like my best was not good enough. I was being beat down. My inner soul was fighting to survive. The fun, happy and loving person that I have always been, where did she go? Why had my partner turned into something that felt so evil? The look on his face said it all. Even when friends would come over they could feel it and see it. I sometimes would feel like someone was watching me through the windows at night. The air in the home seemed to become heavy all the time. I would become unnerved and would go around and close all of the wood blinds. One time I was playing ball with my golden retriever, and I threw the ball into the kitchen. Normally he would always run after the ball and bring it back right away. For some reason on this particular night he seemed to be frightened of the kitchen. He did not want to go get the ball. He acted like someone was in there, and he was frightened. I would know if someone had come into the house, so of course this was silly. I coaxed him into going to get the ball. Wanting to please me, he finally darted a few steps into the kitchen and stopped to look around the corner. Then he darted past the island and looked around that corner again before taking the few more steps to grab the ball. He then quickly scurried back to me. This was the oddest behavior I had ever witnessed from him. I decided to get up and look in the kitchen myself and turned on the light. I found nothing.

I was aware that dogs could see spirits, so it affirmed something tucked in the back of my mind that maybe this house has ghosts. I am hearing impaired so I do not hear sounds that would spook most people. I often wandered around the house without my hearing aids in. I had learned to depend on the dogs as my ears by watching them and their body language if needed to be alerted of something or someone. As I stated in the beginning, I now have pictures of the orbs when I moved. They are some kind of confirmation of what was nagging at me all along. Something to say I was not crazy. We both suspected something was wrong in the house. He would have moments where I felt I could reach the person that I used to know, love, and trust.

We did go as far as trying to use sage in the house. I do not think I ever did it right. I did not know who to contact. I did feel like making any step towards admitting to these feelings would somehow label me as crazy. I think there is something very wrong in and evil in that house. There must be something that was the root to all of this senseless anger and fighting. I feel like I let it

173

win when I moved out. I did not know what else to do. Recently I decided to research the history of Dacula and the land. I found out that a man apparently killed his wife, two of their sons, and then took his own life on October 31st, 1910. For some reason this was not talked about and seemed to have been hidden from Dacula records, but I was able to confirm it in neighboring city papers. Some were shocked that the story of the triple homicide and suicide were never talked about, and it seemed to have been covered up from the history of Dacula. That is the furthest date I can confirm of violence in the area so far.

Dacula has some interesting history, and it is sad to say it seems as though these subdivisions could and have been built right over graves. The thought of that seems so sacrilegious and inhuman. I know right before I moved, it was reported that a man shot and killed his wife, called police, and turned himself in. This was a few streets away in the very same development. I now wonder how much this type of things is going on behind closed doors in the area.

Submitted by Holly, Dacula, Georgia

. . . .

98.
The Mirror

Edgewood, Maryland

I am usually the non-believer in this field until I have "seen it". The fact of the matter is that I've never physically seen this spirit. I recently resided in an apartment right off of Brown Street, and the residential spirit spooked not only me but my fiancé and sister (who came over to babysit while working night shift occasionally.) It started once my fiancé had moved in with my son and I. We would hear small noises. (Nothing to be alarmed about; the house could have been old enough to talk when it got cold.) The TV would come on by itself here and there (harmless,) and doors would be left open within the house. By the time we walked back past it the door would be shut, not slightly closed but shut.

All of this was going on within the first four months of my fiancé moving in. Our family room had elephant shaped tea candle holders lined along the entertainment stand. Somehow they wound up on the floor in a straight line on the floor directly in front of the TV. I could never forget the night my fiancé and I (both drained after coming home from work) sat up to watch a few late night shows. As usual with myself and late night TV I fell asleep. He kept calling me "babe come to bed" over and over again. I started getting a little ticked off with him and shouted "okayyyy. " I started dosing off again when all of a sudden I heard a loud slam coming from the kitchen. It was so loud my heart almost beat out of my chest instantly. It was official that I was up!! I went into the kitchen where I found his cologne lying on the floor next to the wall. I accused him of being a jerk so hard that we began to argue.

My fiancé is not one to swear on his children's lives, but when he swore to me that he did not throw the cologne I had to believe him! In addition, the angle that my bed was located (right behind the bedroom door) there was no way he could have missed

175

everything and hit the wall without standing directly in the doorway! I no longer stay at this house, but I was very freaked out. A few weeks later I was the last to shower, and everyone else was in bed already. I cleared a patch in the mirror (which took up majority of the bathroom wall) to brush my teeth. I turned off the light and went to bed only to find the next morning my mirror was cracked. It was not a stress crack from the neighbor's kids banging against the wall. It was as if someone took a blade of some sort and sliced it from the top left corner down towards the bottom-center of the mirror while staying firmly in its place on the wall (no chips or pieces of glass missing.) I notified the maintenance team, and they came to look at it. His quote "there is no way this happened by itself. " I proceeded to show him how smooth cut the mirror was and reminded him if we had broken this mirror it should show signs of stress or force.

By this time I was spooked and claiming that indeed there was a spirit haunting my apartment. After that I could not stay home alone after dark. No one was ever physically harmed or threatened directly. There were many smaller incidents that happened while living there, but these are the ones that confirmed there was something unknown going on.

Submitted by Nightshifter, Edgewood, Maryland
. . . .

99.

Mistake

Grand Rapids, Minnesota

I lived in a house thirteen miles out of Grand Rapids, MN on River Road. I remember when we viewed the house I got a feeling of doom and gloom, but my husband was totally in love with the place. The floors were all natural oak upstairs in the kitchen and formal living room. When we moved in as much as I tried to make that house a warm and loving place it just was not. We would sit downstairs and watch TV, and we would hear someone walking around upstairs. When we went up there to investigate there was not anyone to be found. There would be times when all of sudden we would all smell something rotten almost like a dead rotting body. Then almost as quickly as we all smelled it, the smell would disappear. We had a pond off of the deck that looked swampier than anything. Anytime we went down there it was creepy like someone was watching you.

One night we had the windows open and heard someone or something walking by our window. We got up to investigate, and as usual we found nothing! A few hours later we both had just dismissed the footsteps thinking it was an animal or our dogs outside. Both of us were drifting off to sleep when we heard a knock at the door. It was not a loud knock but enough to wake us up. I got this enormous feeling of dread and a fear of what was behind the door. I begged my husband not to open the door, but being a typical male he did. Just then a big gust of wind came through our door, and I could not help but feel this was a big mistake. The bedroom next to us started having sounds coming from it like chanting, low mumbling sounds. My daughter who slept in that room refused to sleep in there. She complained that her dolls were scaring her. This went on for weeks on end.

My husband made excuses about it and tried to dismiss it. After a while he got spooked, so we asked a man of the cloth to come out and bless the house. It seemed to help for a while but eventually got worse. The low voices and chanting continued. It was not too long after that our marriage fell apart, and we lost our house and business. I often wonder why that house was haunted and had such a bad vibe. I wonder if that was the reason everything changed. We had two dogs. One died on the road; the other died mysteriously from a heart attack when he was just a puppy. A couple of years later after my husband and I had divorced I moved south of Duluth. I was working there and was staying with a friend that owned a house. One night we were getting ready for bed, and we heard a knock at the door. It was just as strange as the one near Grand Rapids, MN. But this time I convinced her not to answer the door. She looked out of window where she could see the door, and no one was there! After that nothing bad happened. Thank God, so you be the judge.

Submitted by Kay, Grand Rapids, Minnesota

. . . .

100.

Aaron

Aberdeen, Washington

My family had a history of being able to see spirits, so I have learned not to fear them. (Trust me though sometimes I still do.) I was living on Morgan Street in Aberdeen, a block from AJ West. When we first moved in it was just my son and I; his dad was working out of town. I had a computer set up in the front room. It was one of the old, heavy, bulky ones. We were watching TV one night, and a deep male voice came through the computer. My son was scared, so I told him it was just interference from a trucker down on port dock. Over the next couple of days it happened several more times. It was truly scaring him, so I disconnected the computer and put it in the closet in my bedroom. Unfortunately, the voice decided to use my TV next. I could not understand what words were being said. I did not feel it was menacing, but since it was talking to my son (he was only six) and I started to talk back to the voice.

I finally told it "you are frightening my son. I can't understand what you are trying to tell me. So please stop coming here. He is young and scared. Stop coming here!" That ended the voice, but that was not all we had in that house. Our front windows were about six to seven feet off the ground. We were watching TV one night, and I saw a face looking in the window that faced my neighbor's house. Our windows did not line up, so it ruled them out. It was dark, so I could not see clearly, but I went outside to see if there was someone in the walkway between our houses. Nope. The next time I saw the face it was daytime, and I saw him clearly. He was about twelve years old. He was blonde with light eyes and a very young face. He was wearing a baseball hat (not pro but maybe little league.) I went outside again, and he was not there. Now having seen his face I knew he could not have been standing and able to look in my windows that were too high.

I told my neighbor about it, and she called her oldest daughter to come tell me what she had seen. She described the same boy. He had followed her into her house. He did talk to her and told her his name. I do not recall it now for sure, but I want to say Aaron. She asked him why he was there and not in heaven, but he could not remember how he got there. He never talked to me, nor did he ever come into our house. We saw him in our window often over the years we lived there. Now we have a jokester who likes to run up and down our stairs when my son is not home for the night. I wish I could see him, so I could slap him for keeping us awake!

Submitted by Connie, Aberdeen, Washington

. . . .

101.
Reality Check

Shady Point, Oklahoma

I went out to this old bridge to prove to myself that the rumors are false and that the people who said it was haunted were story tellers. Well, I just got to that old bridge, turn off my truck, and waited for the ghost. I waited and waited and waited. I started getting cold, so I reached in my back behind the seat, pulled out my blanket, wrapped up, and I had pain shoot through my head. I had never felt a pain like this in my life. I just turned the key, and my truck started. Then I put it in gear, and I started to drive. My truck turned off, and the head lights went off and on really fast. Then the radio was turning off and on and nothing but static was blasting out the speakers. Then the chill in the truck was so cold. All of a sudden lights came on in the cab of my truck, and the pain in my head was pounding.

I suddenly was overwhelmed with being unhappy and felt emptiness. It was crazy. The truck turned on and head lights would not come on. Then something caught my eye. I saw a foggy misty light green haze that I thought might be headlights coming towards me. I have never been on this road till this night, so I was trying to tell myself it was a car coming. Well, that misty haze started shifting and turning in all directions. Then all of a sudden this mist looked like it was dropping really quickly. Then I could see a complete woman. She was hanging. She was the only thing that was glowing. I saw her plain as day, her feet dangled for a second, and then she was gone. All the sudden my headache was gone. My truck was not flashing all lights off and on. My radio was not off and on any more. I turned my key on, and my truck started right up.

That bridge changed my way of thinking. If a person would have told me what I just told you, I would say they are crazy or they had a wild imagination. I do not have to waste my time writing

181

this if it was not true. I do not care if you believe. I just want to say I will never go back to that bridge. She is very real, and I do not believe children or people with heart problems or breathing problems should go out to this bridge. Please be prepared for a reality check.

Submitted by I will never say there is no ghost, Shady Point, Oklahoma

. . . .

102.
Waiting

I have lived in the same house for twenty years, and I am currently living there but looking for a job and another place to live. My house is on Calapooia Street by the creek, diagonal from the park. I have had many paranormal experiences in this house which have started since I was about seven or eight. I cannot really remember, but I was a child. Whenever I would sing alone in my room I would feel hands on my shoulders or the occasional hug. I knew that that spirit did not mean harm. There are many other spirits in the house, some not quite as friendly. Half misty apparitions can be seen out of the corner of my eyes. Even a shadow has been seen.

Once I was sleeping and got woken up by two hands grabbing my shoulders. Another time I was trying to sleep and felt like I was being watched, so I looked around in my room and saw a glowing red orb at the foot of my bed. I closed my eyes tight and forced myself to go to sleep.

The scariest moment happened a few years ago. When I said some of the spirits were not as friendly I meant some were downright evil (devil/demon maybe.) I have a cat that I treat like a child. I have had her since the second grade, and she still lives to this day. One night I closed my door to my room, and she, my cat, was not in my room. I fell asleep quickly and without problem. In the morning I did not think anything happened, and I got into the bathtub filled with warmish-hot water. I started lowering my back into the water and a white hot burning sensation hurt my back. Immediately I rose out of the tub and started drying myself off. The towel gave off the same burning sensation on my back, and I knew something was wrong. Looking in the mirror (with a second mirror of course) I was able to see my back, and there were long claw marks going down a good length of my back with a bunch of tiny claw marks crisscrossing the long marks.

Since that day activity has gone down to almost nothing, but I could still feel the sensation of being watched and an anticipation like the thing watching is waiting for the perfect moment to hurt me again.

Submitted by Ria, Albany, Oregon

. . . .

103.
The Footsteps

Cleveland, Tennessee

I was born in Cleveland, Tennessee. I spent the first six years of my life there. I remember two different places we lived. The last place I lived was in a house that had the airport runway right in the backyard. The house was white and was by itself at the end of a gravel road. I remember at night you could hear someone walking through the hallway from the bathroom. It sounded as if they had a limp or was dragging one of their feet. The sound would continue on through the dining room, on through the kitchen, and in to the sunroom. Then it just stopped.

The first time we heard it my sister was asleep in my dad's chair. She heard the footsteps and jumped up thinking dad was home (dad was an OTR truck driver.) When she looked no one was there, so she screamed and woke us all up. Mom thought she saw something going out through the sunroom and ran to see what was there. She could not find anything. This continued on most nights if anyone were up late in the living room watching TV, or if company was there. We lived there I think maybe about two years. My dad died there in 1975 from a massive coronary in the big bedroom in the corner of the house. I remember packing to move after his death, and my mom crying saying we would not have to deal with the footsteps anymore.

It was not until years later that I found out from mom when they investigated the history of the house that the owner or person who built it had a stroke in a barn that used to be on the property. From what she told me the barn had caught on fire, and the owner had a stroke trying to put the fire out. Evidently it was this person's footsteps we were hearing at night.

I also remember playing in the yard in a plastic pool dad had brought home, and I saw an elderly woman looking at me and my brothers from the window beside the fireplace in the living room. She did not look menacing or evil, just grandmotherly. It was as if she was making sure we were ok. I saw her several more times over the two years we lived there.

Submitted by Anonymous, Cleveland, Tennessee

. . . .

104.
Doc

Carterville, Missouri

My family and I have lived in this old house in the middle of Carterville since 1993 when I was born. Supposedly, the house was built in 1907 for the first town doctor. However, he died almost as soon as he moved in. Now, considering the time frame, you have to realize, the examination and waiting rooms made up the downstairs and are now converted into a living room and office.

All rooms including kitchen and basement were originally accessible from a central doorway. For thirty or fifty years the house was reserved for the practicing physician. That back story now explains why we affectionately nicknamed our ghost, Doc. Who knows who he really is, if anything more than a series of unexplainable phenomena? Nothing scary or definitive has ever happened really. Just things like creaky stairs or flickering lights, or it seems like if anyone is up too late, things will unexplainably fall off tables and shelves.

None of the doors in the house latch correctly, so they are either wedged shut or locked with a swing lock, and they will open like someone has pushed them, but no one is there. The basement is extremely frightening and obviously the oldest, ugliest, most spider ridden part of the house. We have always said that is where Doc sleeps. It is completely concrete and there is a root cellar in the deepest, darkest, muskiest corner. That is where I have experienced the most activity and the kitchen, being directly above the basement.

One particular time I remember being in the living room and looking directly through the hall out the kitchen window a little while after the sun went down, but having enough light to see with. I saw a man step in front of the window. He was a very solid man in a dark broad suit and circle glasses. However, it did not worry me or make me feel unsafe. A moment later he was gone, and that was it. Whether or not he is real, I just do not think he means us any harm. It has never been a big deal, just interesting.

Submitted by Brittainy, Carterville, Missouri

. . . .

105.

Evil Eyes

Conroe, Texas

I moved to Conroe from Houston when I met my ex-wife back in 2000. We used to live on Gladstell Road. One day we both took a walk down Gladstell towards the 45-freeway. There was an abandoned building which sat at the corner almost directly across from a store. We both took a spot and sat down on top of an old table-like piece of furniture. We were just talking and hanging out. She started taking pictures of me with her little camera. She had this camera where you could snap a photo, pull out the little strip, and it would have a sticky strip on both sides of the small picture which takes a few minutes to develop on its own.

As she was showing me the picture it was developing and you could plainly see this image next to me. It was next to my head on the right side with two evil eyes and a mouth with jagged teeth. You could see the outlining of its head. This image was clearly visible, and it looked evil! We both freaked! All of a sudden we heard a loud slamming sound, and I could see out of the corner of my eye this huge sliding glass door moving to a shut position like someone slammed it hard. That made us jump.

It was the building's back door, and the building was about a hundred and twenty feet away from us on the same property. We walked over to the glass door examining it and opened it, it took a lot of strength to open it. There was no wind, and nobody who could have done this crazy thing. We knew then something other than normal was going on. We looked back at the picture, and the face was still there but fading. By the time we got home the face was completely gone. That was just one story. I have a few more coming about the Conroe area, especially in that little area of Gladstell.

Submitted by Christopher, Conroe, Texas

106.

Not Cool

Bath, New York

I have lived in a house on Geneva Street and have been there just less than two years. There is no doubt in my mind that this house is haunted. I grew up on the Jersey Shore where for whatever reason most houses have activity, so I am a bit more receptive towards these things than my fiancé. Since the day we moved in I have always felt someone right near me or watching me, to the point where my hair stands up. I heard thumps and walking noises from day one, and the old lady would just laugh or pass it off when I told her like I was crazy.

Then one night, we were laying in bed on the second floor and could hear someone walk all the way to the top of the steps and just stop. She was not laughing that time. I would be home alone and hear someone walking in my bedroom while I was downstairs in the front living room. I would also hear it while my fiancé was up there sleeping and it was not her. I have also noticed since I moved to this house I will ALWAYS catch someone out of the corner of my eye standing near me or sitting depending on where I was at the time, and it is a constant thing. I have recently been taking pictures and finding orbs everywhere but mostly in areas where the house is still original, like the basement.

I also put an EVP recorder upstairs in my room, shut the door, and went downstairs for thirty minutes. Upon review of the recording I heard something jump down off of my bed, and about two minutes later I heard my son's bedroom door shut. Nobody was up there or walking in the house. Oh I also felt someone blow on my face and neck when I was in the shower... Not cool.

Submitted by James, Bath, New York

. . . .

107.

The Builder

Mount Pleasant, Pennsylvania

I do not really believe in ghosts, but I can say I have had experiences I could not explain. When I was younger I lived in a town called Mount Pleasant in Pennsylvania. It was a typical small town with lots of old buildings and houses. Being a small older town of course you hear ghost stories, but nobody really believed in that sort of thing. My story starts when I started dating a boy who lived a few streets over from my house. I think his street was called College.

Anyway, we were walking down his street one night, and I noticed an older man staring at us out of a window on the second floor of his house. I asked the boy I was with who the creepy guy was. He said he had never seen him before. He said the house belonged to a doctor, a chiropractor or masseuse or something like that. I noticed the guy a few times staring out of the different windows in the house. I was really shocked the day we saw the guy standing in the yard next to the house. He was wiping sweat off of his forehead with a bandana. My boyfriend said hello and asked him if he lived in the house. I got really freaked out when the guy said "no I don't live here anymore. I did build the place though. Actually helped raise a few of these houses. You kids take care now. " The guy then walked around the back of the house. My boyfriend and I ran down the alley next to the house, and the guy was gone. He may have gone into the house, but we were not sticking around to find out. We never saw the creepy stranger again.

Submitted by ShannonW34, Mount Pleasant, Pennsylvania
. . . .

191

108.
I See Shadows

Fishers, Indiana

Sometimes in my house I see shadows. It has been happening a lot lately. It is starting to freak out my family. Just last night the strangest thing happened, and I need to get it out. I heard some strange banging around downstairs, so my wife and I went to check it out. Nothing was there, so we both went back upstairs. Both of us went back to sleep, but it was not before long that that we woke back up because of other strange banging around. Except this time it was in our room. I turned on the lights and look everywhere for something that might have caused that sound.

Then all of a sudden my wife gasped. I looked up to see she was standing next to her old things from when she was little. She held up one of these statues of an angel that she got from her grandparent when she had her first communion. I noticed at exactly that moment that one of the wings has been broken off of the statue. It was literally broken off of it. We also noticed that we have a pendant of Jesus on our door handle, and the pendant had somehow made its way half across the room. So we think that whatever was downstairs must have followed us up to our room and started mess around up there. We do not know what to do, but we hope it does not get any worse. Wish us good luck!

Submitted by Scared person, Fishers, Indiana
. . . .

109.
Mini Explosion

Solvang, California

When I lived in a condo on Village Lane I always felt scared and uneasy there. I felt like someone was watching me. My upstairs bedroom had a window or loft-like opening where I could look through and see the living room floor beneath. Sometimes I would hear someone walking in the living room and thought it was my son whose room was also upstairs, but no one was there. I would check on him, and he would be sound asleep. Other times I would hear footsteps in the kitchen or a bang like a cupboard closing, but my son was sound asleep. I always chalked it up to neighbors, or the house settling, or whatever even though the sounds were clearly coming from my own unit.

The most undeniable crazy thing that happened though was when I was lying in my bed reading one night, and I heard a loud bang, like a mini explosion. It was coming from the direction of my window. I looked up in time to see a bright light shoot through the window from the outside, and I kid you not, my blinds shot forward as the light pushed through them! It was insane. I looked out the window to see what could have caused that, and there was nothing there. Nothing could have caused that anyway because a light cannot move items, but it did! I moved shortly afterwards.

Submitted by Dee, Solvang, California

. . . .

110.
Dream Or Real

Clarksville, Tennessee

I did not have this experience, but my seven-and-a-half- year-old son who has Autism had a strange experience. We have lived in our home for ten years now, and we live next to a civil war cemetery. I have never felt uneasy inside or outside of our home.

A few nights ago my son was telling his teacher, therapist (and then me later in the day) that he was so tired because he couldn't sleep. This is extremely odd because he usually never gets up in the night. When asked why he explained that the ghosts were being noisy and keeping him up. He explained that he never saw them and their noises were muffled. It may be just a low humming type of a sound from what I understood. I asked him if they were good or bad, and he told me good. Then he got very descriptive and said the bad ones were outside in our backyard by the fire pit. They were tall like the height of our ceilings. They were black and had very long beards.

I talked with him and said if he ever felt frightened, he had to let me know. He has not mentioned this anymore since it happened. It just makes me wonder if he had a dream or if he really saw something.

Submitted by Jessica, Clarksville, Tennessee

. . . .

111.

Never Afraid

Bridgeton, New Jersey

I lived on Walnut Street in Bridgeton for years. The half of the house that I lived in had a ghost in it. I could hear it (a boy) walking up and down the stairs at night. When I first moved in I had my kitchen set up. I was in the living room, and I heard a noise in the kitchen and went out to see what it was. I found one of my chairs pulled out from under the table. One day my neighbor called me and inquired as to what I was doing - rearranging the dishes? I asked "why?" She told me that she heard me making all kinds of noises in the cabinets. I told her that I had just gotten in from work!

Two people actually saw the 'ghost. ' It was a young male, and he was looking for someone. I never saw the 'form,' but I knew he was there on a daily basis. I remember one time I was looking frantically for something I had left on the table. I spoke out loud and said "I am going downtown to run some errands, and when I get back it'd better be on my table!" It was! I lived in that house for several years and was never afraid of the 'form' or 'ghost' that lived there too.

Submitted by Ellen, Bridgeton, New Jersey
. . . .

112.
Lenape Spirit

Warwick, New York

I was alone at Cascade Lake. I passed the lake and started walking upstream along the stream instead of the trail. While dipping my hand upstream from the lake I sensed a lot of presence but did not see anything "supernatural. " On my way back to the parking lot I was away from the creek and was on the main trail next to the lake and before the little meadow that is next to the parking lot.

I was about to take a trail up a little hill on the left (the lake to my right) not too far of a walk from the parking lot. I saw the ghost of what I think was a Lenape man spirit. He ran up to the top of the hill near me. It felt like he heard something (me) approaching and ran to make sure his tribe or clan was safe.

I bowed to him with my hands pressed together (in common prayer pose) at the level of my heart. I got a vibe he felt I respected him. I walked away as he disappeared. It was an amazing experience. I understand this could have all been made up in my head, or maybe I am "crazy". Or maybe I really saw a Lenape ghost.

Submitted by Anonymous, Warwick, New York
. . . .

113.

A Little Girl Ghost

West Covina, California

I moved to West Covina in 2008 into what I thought was a nice quiet house. I was wrong. We have a little girl ghost who looks like the Grudge. She has been seen by everyone who spent the night. She has been photographed a few times. One of my sons has been scratched on his back. My daughters have been grabbed on the arms, shoulders, and legs. We get bruises from nowhere. My husband did not believe us until he saw her himself. He was shocked.

We hear dishes and silverware being moved around. Things get thrown at us. Things disappear from where they were and put into another room. We also have an old man and a woman who we see here and there. One time at night we saw someone walking on our roof that looked like Jeepers Creepers. Then he just disappeared into thin air. We are not the only ones who have seen this in West Covina. No one has lived here more than a year. We have been here six years. We are used to things like this.

Submitted by Dee, West Covina, California

. . . .

114.
Evil Ghost

Greenville, South Carolina

I used to live in a converted barn just off of Anderson Road. I witnessed many events in that home. Some of them are as follows... One day while sitting in the living room I noticed a very heavy shadow of an old man or woman walk across the opposite wall from where I was, I thought someone was outside on the large porch.

I looked, no one was there or on the street out front.

Another time I came home from work one evening and was in the kitchen making a cup of tea. The only light that I had on was a small night light so the kitchen was fairly dark. As I stood facing the counter I heard someone, a man, clearly say hello. I wear a hearing aid in one ear and am deaf in the other so I am not given to auditory hallucinations. I jumped and turned with my fists up and looked to see no one.

I lived alone and the house was very large I knew no one should be there. After a moment I said I can hear you, but I can't see you, so please don't scare me like that anymore. Nothing else happened that night.

On another occasion I was in my room sleeping when I was awakened by sounds of crashing and banging around somewhere in the house. There was no way I was going to open my door to look as every horror movie starts with someone doing something stupid like that.

I just sat up in bed and waited to see what would happen next. I fell asleep waiting. The next morning nothing was amiss. There is also a room over the kitchen with a private staircase leading up to it. I hated that staircase and kept the door to it closed at all times.

It gave me a bad feeling. Everyone that came over had the same feeling about it. I later found out that the house was originally the barn to a dairy farm. The house is across the street. The original owners were a family named Scott.

There were parents and two children, a boy and a girl. The siblings were playing next to the barn one day in the 1930s when the brother "accidentally" almost chopped his little sisters head off with a scythe used for mowing hay by hand.

She recovered but spent the rest of her life in a state hospital. The young man grew up and married. The father passed away and the mother eventually converted the barn into a home for herself. She was said to be a mean spirited woman who disliked children and spent all of her days picking weeds out of her yard and warning kids to stay off of her lawn.

The son and his wife and children moved into the small house. Mrs. Scott lived in the barn until the day she died. I know the son's wife divorced him for being a drunkard and a wife beater. She left him and the children and moved to New York.

I was friendly with the couple that now occupied the home across the street and was not surprised to learn that no one ever lived in that home for long. I stayed for a year and I loved it but couldn't sleep there.

The house was too active at night so I moved.

Submitted by Karen, Greenville, South Carolina
. . . .

115.

Odd House

I lived in Independence in a house on Main Street. The house was beautiful, inviting and wonderful while the sun was up. When it went down at night the entire house became odd. Doors would open and then close themselves. If you specifically closed a door, you would find it wide open a second later. Not all doors however. There were a few very odd rooms in the house. One had no clear purpose, apparently for storage. It had a very small rusty window in it that we could never open. The strange thing was that there was a room within that room with a small door. The inner room was finished but had no windows, and no way out from the inside. Whatever temperature the house sat at, that room was so cold you could see your breath. The doors to this room would open and close by themselves.

One day while my mother, brother, and I were upstairs, we heard this awful wrenching sound and a thud. In the strange room the window was wide open. We were scared but thought we were being silly. We attempted to close the window, but it was hard. We had to use a hammer to move the latch back in place. Five minutes later we were sitting quietly, and we heard the wrenching noise again. When we went to look the doors in the room were both wide open as was the window. There were more odd rooms in the house. Another for storage with nails pounded through the ceiling. Once again this room always stayed freezing. There was another odd room in the basement which was padlocked from the outside. There were odd stains in the cement floor and a mattress against the wall. The oddest room, however, was the room behind the fridge. Where our fridge was we could see a boarded-up door. The house clearly had a large room there as there was a large spot for it. There were stairs that led up to a blank wall where there used to be passage from this room to the outside. We were instructed to never try and enter the room. This piece of information I learned only days ago.

The people who lived there before us left in the middle of the night. They left EVERYTHING THEY OWNED. There was food in the fridge, pictures on the walls, keepsakes, and so on. They said they wanted NONE of it and told the landlord not to contact them ever again. Now, why would they do that if there was nothing wrong with that house? I am trying to find any information I can on this house. I moved out four years ago, and I have nightmares very often of being trapped in the house, digging through possessions that do not belong to my family. With the information on the old owners, I am very frightened about these dreams. They are specific, and sometimes they are of the house in its original form built 1914.

Submitted by Cecilia, Independence, Oregon
. . . .

116.
Blue Figure

Quincy, Massachusetts

Me and my cousin were watching TV at our grandparents house in Wollaston when all of a sudden it turned off but we thought nothing of it until it did it again and again and then went into a storm warning (it was a peaceful summer night). After the TV kept freaking out and neither of us had the clicker that's when it got weirder. We heard a noise that sounded like chains against the floor coming down the stairs. When we looked over we saw a blue figure coming down and it stood right behind the couch. It then proceeded to turn the corner and when it came back out it was just a blue ball floating that floated across the doorway and into the fire place where it disappeared.

About 4 years later I was coming home and had to put the keys back in the kitchen (before I went back to my house across the street) as I turned to go back outside I stopped and said "if you are here show yourself" (which I had done on occasion since my first experience). Nothing happened so I went to turn around until In the doorway across the kitchen where the dining room was started to look blue (almost as if someone was watching television but it was too late and no one was up) this immediately reminded me of the blue figure with my cousin and as I started to walk towards the light which was getting brighter something appeared. I took 2 or 3 steps into the kitchen when all of a sudden a smaller female shadow figure leaned out from the door way and stood across from me. My body froze and the shivers I got was like nothing I've ever felt before. After being frozen stiff for a second staring at this figure I turned around and walked fast out the door and back to my house to call my cousin who had just been talking with his girlfriend about our first experience. There has been no sighting since.

Submitted by Bill, Quincy, Massachusetts

117.
Two Young Kids

Zavalla, Texas

Me and my young family used to live about 3 miles outside of Zavalla in a small 3 bedroom house just off of hwy. 147 in the early 1990s. Over the course of about 8 years strange things would happen to us. Sometimes we would wake up in the middle of the night to find that the lights in the kitchen or living room would be on.

One night I woke up and noticed the light in the kitchen was on. So I got up and started walking down the hall to turn it off. As I got to the end of the hall I stopped short thinking I was going to walk into someone but there was no one there. My wife was in the bedroom and both kids were asleep. Several different times things would come up missing like car keys or the remote control for the TV.

We could search the entire house for these things and they would turn up laying in plain sight on the coffee table or some other place where they would have been easily found. It got to the point to where whenever we would be trying to find something my wife would say out loud "please put it back! " and we would find it shortly after in plain sight.

One morning our 3 year old son came to me and my wife to tell us about two young kids that he had seen standing at the end of his bed. He gave us a lot of detail about what they were wearing and such.

To this day he remembers that night because it really spooked him. Other times we would all be out in the yard and you could hear footsteps inside the house. The house was not a very old house so I don't think the house itself was haunted but the land was. We never lived in fear or ever felt threatened while we lived there. I have never lived in a place that I have had those types of experiences before or after.

Submitted by Charles, Zavalla, Texas

. . . .

118.
Scary House

Hempstead, Texas

In 2012 my husband and I lived in a little house that was situated on the corner of 369 and only a short distance from the fairgrounds, there is another newer log cabin style house that is also on the grounds.

Immediately after moving in I experienced feelings that something wasn't quite right there but was never able to put my finger on what it was. Occasionally I would get cold chills whenever I stepped into the little hallway that separated the kitchen from the living room but really never gave it any thought until one day right before we got ready to move.

I had just come in from outside and was leaning up against the doorway that separated the living room from the hallway when I saw a spool of thread that sat on a shelf in the hallway (that faced south) come off the shelf, turn and fly east into the kitchen where it flew all the way until it hit the kitchen cupboards. I was so freaked out over it I left until my husband came home.

I then picked up the spool of thread and tried to debunk what I saw by knocking it off the shelf with my hands to see if I could simulate what I had witnessed. I never could get the spool of thread to even roll to the east, when I hit it off the shelf it would only go forward heading south.

To try to hit it on the side it would hit up against the shelf and fall to the floor . I tried for a good half an hour until my husband told me to just accept what I had seen and leave it at that. I was really glad to finally move.

Submitted by Pam, Hempstead, Texas

. . . .

119.
A Little Girl

Bardwell, Kentucky

One night as I was walking to visit my friend, I noticed a shadow moving to the left of me. Being a resident of the town, I was in knowledge that there is no such paranormal activity around the area. Although after that night I may have changed my mind. I thought I heard a whisper, but I showed no attention to it. Then as I got closer to my friend's house, I heard her call my name. Relieved at this I hurried down the road. It was dark outside, but I had never really been scared until then. When I approached her house the porch light was not on, and neither were any indoor lights. Appalled at this, I knocked on the door. I had thought maybe she was playing a prank on me and was going to pop out from behind a tree at any moment.

Nevertheless I began walking back home when I heard her say my name again. I then turned around to see nothing. When I turned back around I think I turned completely white at the sight. A little girl was standing not ten feet away from me. She was dressed in all white, and her finger was perched on her lips as if shushing me. She pointed behind me, and I hesitated to turn around when I heard footsteps. Then as I turned around, my friend was running towards me asking where I was going. When I whipped back around the little girl was gone. I never told my friend about the sight in fear that she would make fun of me or claim I was lying. I have never seen the girl again, and to this day I watch my back if ever to travel down the road at night.

Submitted by Anonymous, Bardwell, Kentucky

. . . .

120.
My Parents' Trailer

Ashdown, Arkansas

My parents owned a trailer by Millwood Lake in Ashdown, Arkansas. While my parents lived in the trailer they would wake up to the bed shaking. They experienced this a few times. After my parents moved out my sister moved into the trailer. She slept in the same bedroom that my parents had. The room would get real cold, and she had trouble warming the room. She would see a dark shadow come out of the closet and crawl by the bed on several occasions. A few times she would try to open the door, and someone was pulling the door on the other side, so she could not open the door.

She said she started cursing at it to let her in, and it just let go as she was pulling on it. Her grandson who was only about three at the time came running out of the bedroom. He said he saw a man in there. She would keep bath toys for when her granddaughter stayed with her hanging in the bathtub, and several times the toys would be knocked down into the tub. Once she was lying on the couch asleep, and she heard the kitchen cabinets opening and closing. She woke up and went and shut the cabinets. She fell back to sleep and woke up to something scooting across the kitchen floor. She looked in the kitchen, and a stool was in the middle of the kitchen. She lived there for about two years and experienced other things in this nature.

Submitted by Sandy, Ashdown, Arkansas

. . . .

121.
Following Them Here
Hyde Park, Pennsylvania

We rented a garage apartment in Hyde Park, PA. Our TV volume would go all the way up on its own. Sometimes we came home to our TV on full volume on static, and our bathroom sink would be running. I had tugs on my shirt as if a little kid was trying to get my attention. Once I was home alone in the shower, and I could hear loud persistent knocking on the door. When I checked nothing was there. I would hear my kids call my name from their bedroom, but when I would go in, they were asleep. We had so many occurrences through the years that we lived there.

We have since moved. When our son was two he said he would talk to PJ in our basement/garage. I tried to check into local history, but no one knew of someone named PJ. I would be woken up hearing one of our nephews screaming. I would wake up my husband to go check. He would tell me that the kids were all playing video games quietly in bed, and the kids said no one had made a sound. At the same time my brother lived in Leechburg, and he and his girlfriend experienced the same occurrences before we started to. I wondered if whatever was in their house followed them to our apartment. Since we bought our house nearby we have not had anything happen. Thank goodness!

Submitted by , Hyde Park, Pennsylvania
. . . .

122.
A B&B On Main Street
Fredericksburg, Texas

We were staying at a B&B on Main Street. It was very nice, and we loved the room. We had popped by throughout the day to drop off things we bought and never saw anyone. That night I was sound asleep. Then at 2:00 am footsteps in the hall woke me up. I thought it was just someone going to their room. Then it sounded like they were pacing in front of our room. I figured they were waiting for somebody. Then I started hearing what I thought was whispering, but I realized it was too even, that it was someone breathing. It was very loud as if they were right beside me.

Then they started messing with the locks on our door. At this point my eyes were open and looking at the door. Right above our door was one of those small rectangle windows with a little curtain over it. When you were lying down you could see under the curtain. While I was looking at the door because our locks were being messed with a head appeared in that little window. I could not see any features, but I could definitely make out that it was a head looking into our room. I turned on the lamp, and everything stopped. Needless to say, we were gone in minutes and never saw anyone in the hall.

Submitted by Crystal, Fredericksburg, Texas
. . . .

123.
A Trinidad Brick

Trinidad, Colorado

I have heard so many stories from my family members (my aunts, uncles, and grandparents) about this house on Tillotson Road. The one that I always remember is when my grandmother, grandfather, my mother, and my aunt went to visit the old house. My grandma grew up in it with her eleven other siblings. My mom was like four, and my aunt was two. My grandmother took a Trinidad brick and got in the car, and they were about to drive away.

Out of nowhere there was this man next to my grandma's window on the passenger's side. He dressed like a cowboy. He yelled "you can't take that brick. " He said "this here is my property. " He was holding this big knife. He yelled "I'm calling the sheriff down here," and he talked and dressed like from another time. My grandma threw the brick out of the car and drove. She looked back, and he disappeared.

The creepy thing is that after my family moved out, the house got bought out and is used for auto parts and junk cars. No one lives there, and no one lived there on that day that they went. The man said he was the owner, but no one lived there or owned it.

Submitted by Shayleen, Trinidad, Colorado

. . . .

124.
Poor Little Boy

Glasgow, Kentucky

A few months ago my wife, children and I were riding down 68-80, and we saw this little boy standing on the side of the road all alone. We pulled over and stopped to help him. When my wife and I got out of the car the little boy took off running. He ran right in the middle of the road, and this semi was coming towards him. We were yelling at him trying to get him to come back over to us for safety, but he just stood there and stared at us.

The man that was driving the semi later told me that he too had seen this little boy in the middle of the road. The trucker pushed his brakes trying to prevent from running over this poor little innocent child. My wife and I did not know what to do. We thought that this child's life was about to end just like that. My wife got in the car and told my children to close their eyes, so that they would not have to see this horrific accident. The trucker was still applying his breaks trying to prevent from running over the little boy. However, it looked as if he were too late. Right as the trucker approached the little boy, he vanished.

Submitted by Bobby Joe, Glasgow, Kentucky
. . . .

125.
The Officer

Warrenton, Virginia

We grew up in a new home just off Rt. 605. I believe the road was Rt 626. The house had a Civil War Officer in it. He was often spotted by my siblings and parents. He enjoyed moving and reading the local newspaper and turning the water on and flushing the toilets. We could hear him often at night pacing up and down the hallway. If my bedroom door was open, he would stand at the foot of my bed like he wanted conversation. If I spoke he would disappear in smoke.

My brother was getting a glass of water one night in the kitchen, and someone behind him said they would like a glass too. He filled the second glass with water, turned to offer it to his sister, and the officer went up in smoke. This house has been sold multiple times and always back on the market within 6-8 months each time. I think others have seen this officer!

Submitted by , Warrenton, Virginia

. . . .

126.
Tapping In The Wall

Visalia, California

I used to live in some duplex style apartments in Visalia. It was on East Laura right off Ben Maddox right behind Rite Aid. When I first moved in nothing strange really happened at first. Then things would happen little by little. I had a strange experience when I was using the bathroom in the master bedroom. As I was about to leave the bathroom, the light just turned off by itself. I thought the bulb burnt out because I had messed with the light switch, and it would not turn on. When I went in there a few days later to use it again I turned the light switch to on, and it worked just fine. I never liked sleeping in that room even though it was mine. I always got a weird feeling being in there. I would only use that bathroom on certain occasions when the other was occupied.

More and more creepy stuff started to happen. I used to sleep in my son's room with the TV on because I had this uneasy feeling that I was not alone. Well, one night as I was trying to go to bed, the light immediately turned off and then on again in less than a second. My eyes were closed, but I felt the light go away from my eyelids and back on. Sometimes I felt my mind was playing with me until something else happened in my son's room. He used to stack his Legos up on the dresser when he used to stay the night. One night I was sound asleep when I heard a crash. I immediately woke up and saw the Legos had fallen. I looked at them in disbelief and went back to sleep. I probably did not get so freaked out because I was half asleep when I awoke.

Another time when my son was taking a bath I went to watch TV, so he could play with his toys a little bit before I took him out. When I went back in to check on him he was staring at me crying with tears running down his face. I asked "what's wrong?" He said he saw something and that it growled at him. I thought it was his imagination because he was only three years old. Then he told me

213

that he did not want me to leave him alone in the tub, so I took him out. My girlfriend and her kids used to stay the night. One night while I was asleep my girl woke up to a loud crash. I did not immediately wake, but she did. When she did her three-year-old son was standing next to her side scared. She woke me and said "someone was trying to break in. " I went to check and when I reached the bathroom the curtains were knocked down. This was when I became freaked out and got the feeling this place was haunted.

Whenever me and my girl would watch TV in the living room at night every once in a while we could hear as if someone was bouncing a rubber ball on the walls of the kitchen. I always thought it was the neighbor's kids, but it was strange because it did happen in the middle of the night. It sounded as if they were not bouncing against the wall, but almost like if you dropped a rubber ball on the floor and not directly at the wall. It was freaky. It started happening more often because the living room was where we spent most of the day. It started to happen in the day time and at night. My girl was freaked out, and I was too but tried not to acknowledge it.

One night we even heard tapping on the walls in the kitchen at 1:00 am as we were watching TV. I thought it was the neighbors messing with me, so I started to tap back. When I started tapping back the tapping came from everywhere in the kitchen, all over the place. I even put my head to the wall to listen, but the tapping moved to different parts of the kitchen. That was when I decided to stop. I was a little intrigued and a little frightened at the same time. I knew that this could potentially be a bad spirit because worse things started to happen. My girlfriend and I would fight a lot. We had a lot of arguing and name calling.

I eventually moved out, and I am happy to say none of that stuff happens at my new place. I think it was mainly the apartment for the most part. If anyone reads this and is living there now or know

214

someone who does, then I would love to hear some experiences if there are any. May god protect and bless you if strange things are happening. I am glad I am not there anymore. My girlfriend and I felt a strange presence there and sensed it may have been evil.

Submitted by Anonymous, Visalia, California

. . . .

127.
Horrible Smell

Belton, Missouri

I moved into a brand new home in Belton, MO. I was surprised to find that it appeared to be haunted. The entry way chandelier (which has five bulbs in it) would flash off and on or not turn on for days and then suddenly start working again. You can clearly hear walking around in the attic (also heard by guests in the house). Ceiling fans would suddenly make very loud noises in the night just long enough to wake you up. We heard knocking around the bedroom walls at night. A few weeks ago I was videotaping a bright light in the sky in the middle of the night and taped what looks like a ghost flying by my camera phone. (I slowed it down to take a look and it is clearly seen in the video.) One time there was a horrible gritty dust that was throughout the house that my husband and I could hardly breathe.

Another time there was a horrible smell coming from the attic that made it impossible to be in the living room. You might think "well, you just had an animal up there, and it probably died. " That might be except I had the attic inspected, and the fluffy insulation had not been disturbed in any way. The funny thing is my daughter (who suffers from asthma and is also extremely sensitive to smells) was not affected in anyway by the dust or smell incidents. The smell was so putrid that my husband and I had to put an air cleaner in the living room and stay in the bedroom because it was so overpowering, but my daughter could smell nothing.

My daughter did start suffering from seizures after moving into this house. After much prayer, the seizures have stopped. I myself have had multiple falls with some severe and permanent injuries. I have also suffered many financial setbacks which continue until this day. I have recently started doing research on the Cass County Burn District from the Civil War. All of Cass County was

216

affected as houses were burned to the ground, and God only knows what else happened to the women and children that were here when their men were off fighting in the war on one side or the other.

In Cass county, I read in from the Historical Society that only one person voted for Lincoln in Cass County. This area has a very interesting history, and I wonder sometimes if my neighbors are having similar problems. All the homes are new in my subdivision, and it was nothing more than cow grazing here before the homes were built. I plan to do more research on this area to see what happened on this land before that. Oh yes, and the ghost picture resembles a short stocky woman with long thick curly hair.

Submitted by Jewely, Belton, Missouri
. . . .

128.

Old Brown Jugs

Elkhart, Illinois

Many years ago my family farmed an old farmstead, and we lived in the house between Mt. Pulaski and Elkhart. My dad was a non believer who preferred to explain everything away to a logical explanation. The story on the farm was about a hot tempered man that owned the farm. He was from a very wealthy Kentuckian family. Old money, they raised purebred horses and sold them to race. He raised horses but also farmed. This was back in the 1800s. He got into a fight with a man and killed him because he was trespassing on his land. The family kept him from getting hanged and loosing the farm. He was an alcoholic and when we moved in there were brown jugs everywhere. The basement had a cellar and part of it had later on been made into a basement. In one part was a door where in the 1940s and 1950s (and maybe even in the 1960s) coal was delivered to heat the house. It was a spooky dark place, and every time I would go down there to do laundry I would get the feeling someone was watching me.

When you went up the stairs there was a door to go outside, turn left, and go up two more steps to go upstairs into the kitchen. Many countless times we would be in the kitchen or sitting in the living room, and all of us would hear someone open the back door, go downstairs, move stuff around like they were looking for something, then walking up the stairs, and go out the back door. We kept that back door locked and chained. No one used that door. As always dad would get up to investigate, and no one would be there and nothing touched. It was not until we learned of the history of the house and family that we came to the conclusion that the old man was looking for his brown jugs even after death.

Submitted by Nedra, Elkhart, Illinois

. . . .

129

A Beautiful House With The Biggest Trees

Hilliard, Ohio

I do not know if you believe in ghosts, but as a kid I lived at a house on Hilliard Rome Road. It was built across the street in 1947 then moved on Virginia Military property. My parents bought the house on April 1st, 1999. I was ten, my brothers thirteen and fifteen. First project was painting. We noticed crosses above the doors jammed between the door moldings and drywall and a bottle of holy water. My mother and stepdad had five Dobermans that always seemed to be staring at the walls and looked afraid. The second thing that happened was that there was something running up and down the halls, and every so often we heard heavy footsteps. In the back yard it felt like you were being watched all the time. The third was antiques would not just fall but take flight about five or six feet across the room and hit my mom.

An old clock (Big Ben) flew one night, and I had set a Pepsi bottle down on a foot stool, and it flew up and over on top of my stepdad to hit my mom again. Our male Dobe who was about 140 lbs was growling at the end of our long hallway and started attacking nothing. Then something had hit our dog. It ran at us, so my brothers and I got our dogs and sat in the snow waiting for our parents to get back home. My TV in my bedroom would turn on and off by itself. When we moved out was the best day of all of our lives even though it was a beautiful house on an acre of land. The biggest trees on Hilliard Rome Road were in our yard, but the experiences were too much for us to live with. I too did not believe until we moved in that house.

Submitted by Kevin, Hilliard, Ohio

. . . .

130.

Scary Woman

Wichita Falls, Texas

About a year ago my husband and myself rented a house on Kemp. Right next to the tax place. We were expecting our first child at the time. In the living room there was a painting that had been left behind. It gave us the creeps but we never thought much of it until we started having weird dreams. The most vivid dream I remember was being outside with my dog going to see what my husband and a cousin were doing by the "back yard" (it was very tiny) , and as I'm walking back there this woman with shoulder-length brown hair and a dead face was walking up like she was walking towards the tax place but she gave me the coldest stare.

It woke me up, and to this day still gives me chills. I also remember two other instances. The first I woke up at around 2 that morning to pee and remember smelling the smell of cigarette smoke so strong.

Neither my husband nor I smoke, however the walls were yellowed so obviously someone who used to live there smoked. I thought this was very odd. Second, and this scared me so bad at the time; my husband was a pizza delivery driver and I stayed at home. It was around 11 or so at night, I had been cleaning house waiting on him to get home and I had just gotten done getting a load of laundry done so I was going to take the dog out. I turned off the laundry room light, made sure the back door was closed, then turned off the kitchen light and made my way outside.

I was outside for maybe 10 minutes max and I come inside to the laundry room light turned on. The switch had been flipped up and the blinds to the door were shaking. I high-tailed it out of there and sat on the porch until my husband got home which luckily wasn't long. I found it super creepy.

Submitted by Jamie, Wichita Falls, Texas

. . . .

131.
Foot Steps

New Deal, Texas

My family moved to New Deal my freshman year of high school. I never saw anything wrong or felt it was "haunted" until my senior year of high school. It was December and I was up late in my house wrapping presents.

My little sister had just came home from band and we were the only ones awake. We were standing in the dining room when we heard what sounded like feet heavily trotting on the roof back and forth, back and forth.

It seemed to stay only above where we were standing. Every time it would step about where my shoulder ended, it would turn around and go back to where her shoulder was as if to only step above us. We both didn't say anything, we just stared at each other afraid.

Then we heard what sounded like women's high heels or men's dress shoes walking in our kitchen which had ceramic tile. We both left everything as is and ran to her room. That night when I started falling asleep I had my eyes closed and was close to unconsciousness when I heard the door open and felt somebody lay something on my bed.

I thought someone came in so I sat up and the door was cracked open just a bit, then it violently slammed shut as if someone was on the other side and had yanked it towards them. I was so afraid.

My other sister said one day she was home alone and digging through my closet and two children were chasing each other and ran straight into my wall and disappeared.

My mother has heard kids in the dining room laughing and talking once and she kept hollering at us to 'come here' and became angry when we didn't hear her thinking we were ignoring her. She came into the back room and said "who was in the dining room and ignored me when I called them then ran when I came in there? " none of us were in the dining room.

Another time my mom thought my dad came home because she heard men's feet heavily walking in the game room and when she went to look my dad still wasn't home.... Neither were any of us.

Submitted by Anonymous, New Deal, Texas

. . . .

132.
Covered Over

Sylva, North Carolina

I lived in a house in the Wyahuta area several years ago. I only stayed in the house three weeks. The things that were happening just started to become too much. Some friends and I started cleaning the house up getting it ready to move in to. We left, went to town, got dinner, and came back. We returned to find large amounts of horse flies dead all over the place along with the smell of rotten meat. We left, returned the following day, cleaned and moved in. I know this sounds stupid! Why move in? The thing was my friends and I at the time were into searching for answers to the unknown.

As time went on we all had pets to die. At night every night the sounds of laughter from a man and a woman could be heard throughout the house followed by running footsteps. One night my friends and I were standing out by the cars. About thirty feet away from the house we could see inside through the large plate five by seven window. My buddy's little dog started barking sounding as if it was chasing someone or something through the house.

We turned to look at the window just as a white light the size of a dinner plate floated through the living room and up into the ceiling. We ran inside and were overcome with the smell of rotten meat. The next day while my friends were out I went to the owner's house to talk to them about what was happening and wanted any information they could give. They only told me that they would never go to the house. They said I would have to bring the rent money there and that they had someone that would go out and make repairs if needed.

A couple of days later a large rust colored stain appeared on the ceiling in the bedroom. I took down the tiles to discover that the attic entrance had been purposely covered over. Well, my friends and I went up into the attic and found a shell casing from a 45-cal, some old boxes of books and whatnots. Things really got worse after this. We would wake to find all the windows and doors open. Needless to say, we started moving out the next day.

Submitted by Someone New, Sylva, North Carolina

. . . .

133.
Our First Home

Mcallen, Texas

Our experience was in McAllen at the time a new subdivision off Benson Road on 44th ln. We were in our first time home, wonderful and delighted to be in our first home, not only our first home but the model home so it was gorgeous.

Shortly after we moved in my daughter started having terrible nightmares and did not want to sleep in her room. To make her more comfortable we redid her room paint and all. Never the less it didn't work.

I started to have nightmares, at times noises of someone trying to break in got to the point I called 911 three times. They found no evidence of anything. That summer my mother flew in from out of state for a week.

She stayed in my daughter's room, we never told her what we were experiencing because we didn't want her to think we were out of our minds. Low and behold the first morning she stayed at the breakfast table she said, Shelley I don't want to alarm you but something is wrong with your house. Last night something was grabbing my ankles and I heard scratching on the wall.

She said I'm not frightened but this is my grand daughters room, you need to get your house blessed. Shortly after my mother left it got worse. My kitchen cabinets opened and all slammed shut at the same time, company started seeing a shadow person in my kitchen. And on one occasion my daughter's 10th birthday guests got physically ill and nauseous.

They described having a pressure in their head like a terrible headache. My husband and I started fighting unbelievably, anger started to be an everyday occurrence. We had gotten to a point it became physical, we were attacking each other.

Our home was a corner home and two cars drove through our back fence almost going through our master bedroom. That was the last straw. We put our home on the market and could not sell it after two contract renewals.

Ultimately we abandoned our dream home. I can report we are doing fantastic now and know what was happening in that house was out of our control! We have often wanted to go back and talk with the current owners to see if they have had any experiences.

The positive that came out of it is we go to church more regularly and pray every day.

Submitted by Shelley, Mcallen, Texas

. . . .

134.

Never Ending Hallway

Gulf Shores, Alabama

Two years ago, my family and I were visiting Gulf Shores for two weeks. While we were there we made the decision to go to Fort Morgan (which is a brilliant place.) While we were there the area had a kind of eerie feeling to it. I had chills most of the time we were there. The last area we visited was a long hall to the right of the entrance. This hall already has a creep factor as it is only wide enough for one person at a time, covered in graffiti, and seems never ending. The hall seems to go on for what seems like forever. If you do not have a flashlight, do not even plan on trying to go in. The hall has a good bit of turns and gets darker with each turn.

My cousin and I decided to try and see what was at the end of the hall. Being this was our first trip, we had failed to equip ourselves with flashlights. We decided to try and use a phone flashlight and attempt to endure the creepy hall. As we got around the first turn, I began getting chills and almost every hair on my neck and arms stood up, but we carried on anyways. As we got around the third turn, our makeshift flashlight did little to illuminate the impending darkness of the tunnel, both physical and metaphorical.

Now, I am not a claustrophobic person, but I have never felt more suffocated in a small place than in that hall. I had to immediately leave due to the fact that it felt as though multiple beings were pressed against me. I did not want to jump to conclusions and check this off as ghosts, but I can find no other reason as to why I experienced this feeling. I am 100% positive that something is residing in that hallway, and it certainly is not looking to make you feel welcome.

Submitted by Taylor, Gulf Shores, Alabama

. . . .

135

Loud Whispers

Rio Vista, Texas

I have always had weird paranormal activity around me since before I can remember. I was young, but this particular moment in time scared me the most. It started when I was about thirteen or fourteen. I lived on Pavilion just a few houses down from the Legion. I did not feel safe. It felt like something did not want us there. It made me always feel uncomfortable. I shared a room with my little sister Cheyenne. We would always leave our door open at night because she was afraid, and we both felt safer that way. When we would lie down, and she fell asleep late at night it would sound like someone was messing with the kitchen cabinet doors. I would try to ignore it. Often if you glanced out of the door, you could see multiple shadows passing through the kitchen. There would also be a shadow that would pass in front of our door. It would not stay. It moved fast, but it was quite large, and it scared me. It gave off this bad feeling. This happened almost every night.

After a while everyone left to go somewhere, and I chose to stay home alone. It was the middle of day. I thought it would be fine, but instead I kept hearing doors slam. I have heard it before but thought it was nothing. I was alone, so I walked into the kitchen. From there you can see every single door in the house. I watched and not one moved, but the sound did not stop. It got louder in different sides of the house. It scared the hell out of me, and I ran outside and sat on the porch. I told mom and dad when they came home, but she said it was my imagination. I thought maybe she was right. Then we moved to CR 1202 shortly after. Things started getting bad again. I could feel something always around me in that trailer, but I was not the only one. One my little sister now felt it too. It was at its worst in the room we slept in. In the corner at the foot of my sister's bed something was almost always there. You could not see it, but the feeling was so strong. It was

228

scary. I would hear voices and quiet whispers now and then. My bed when I slept a lot of times it would shake. I know that sounds crazy, but it did. I would just cover my face and ignore it. It was dramatic like in the movies.

Every now and then I would try and talk to it, and things would slowly move in my room. My sister soon pretty much moved out of room and onto the couch. I asked her why one day, and she said she was scared but would not give me a reason. I soon noticed there was more than one 'something. ' It was still that scary strong spirit, but at times I felt something small. It was like when I would talk to it; it felt peaceful. It was the 'someone' who sat in the corner. One day I had my younger uncle come stay the night with me, and he slept in my little sister's bed because she would not. We were just about go to sleep when the TV came on by itself to a fuzzy screen. It was really loud, and it scared me. My uncle yelled at me and asked if I played on the remote, but I quickly noticed it sitting on the computer desk. It made us nervous, but we ignored it.

These things kept happening, and shortly after I had my best friend Elisha stay the night with me. It was bedtime, and we were sitting in my room, and she asked if we could sleep in the living room. I asked why, and she told me she did not like being in my room or sleeping on my little sister's bed. She asked me if I ever felt like something was watching me. I told her yes. I know exactly what she was talking about. She said it scared her, so I agreed to leave the room. As we started to leave there was a loud crash like all the dishes fell, but nothing had even moved, so we ran to my brother's room to sleep. He was passed out, so we curled up next to him and shut the door. It did not even take ten minutes before you could hear loud footsteps running in the hall from my room to my brother's and what sounded like hands hitting his door. I looked at Elisha she was hiding her face. Then there was a loud whisper that has never been so clear as it called my name. I thought I was crazy. At this moment my brother lifted up and looked at us and said "did you hear that?" I said "what?" He did not answer me, and he laid back down without a word back to sleep.

The next morning he asked us why we were in his bed. We told him, and he remembered nothing. I was then fifteen. I met a boy, and he lived on Casa Vista. One day I went over to his house, there was this loud whisper. Again I thought "no way. It's not even the same house. " I asked my boyfriend what he heard. He said "it almost sounded like it was saying your name. " I got really scared, and we told his mom. She told us we were crazy. We told his dad and little brother, and they said they have been hearing things too lately. It got bad, and they ended up moving houses. It never really stopped, but now if I choose to ignore these things, it seems to help and happen a lot less. That is my story.

Submitted by Dessira, Rio Vista, Texas

. . . .

136.

Over The Top

Twentynine Palms, California

My husband and I lived on the base back in 1991 in Twentynine Palms. I had the worst dreams and saw so many things, and so did my husband. We are lucky our kids were not bothered. When my husband was deployed I was there alone, so my cousin came from Arizona. I remember this like yesterday. My cousin and two of her friends wanted to watch 'The Exorcist,' and I said "no way. I'm not watching it!" They said they would sit by me, so I would not get scared. Well shortly into the movie I could not do it. They kept saying "oh come on. " I said "please turn it off. " I was sitting on the sofa with my cousin's two friends and my cousin. Then the TV stand slid to the right, and the coffee table in front of us went to the left. The noise it made on that non-carpeted floor was horrifying. We ran outside, and the neighbors looked at us like we were crazy. We asked the neighbors "did you feel that? Was that an earthquake?" They said they felt nothing. He also asked his wife, and she said she did not feel anything. We asked the other neighbors, and no one felt anything, nor was there a report the next day on the news.

We lived where our backyard was to the colonel base commander. We were the second house on that corner. I do not recall that address or housing area, but I wish we stayed in our cute little apartment in town because of having to wake up in the middle of the night going to Catholic Church parking lot for peace. Oh yes, we had the house blessed by the catholic priest on base. He said with us both not being catholic our marriage was doomed, and it most likely would not work. He was right; things got worse. I left. I went back to Arizona and left that creepy haunted house! I have many stories of this place, but watching the movie that night took it over the top!

Submitted by Cherie, Twentynine Palms, California

137.
Godsend

Xenia, Ohio

My husband and I were looking for a house to buy in Xenia in 1977. We found a beautiful old house on S. Detroit that was being sold by an old man in a nursing home. We went to look at it and loved it. However, there was a weird cold feeling on the stair steps going upstairs and a very heavy feeling in one of the bedrooms. We just blew it off as being a little paranoid. We loved the house and wanted to buy it! I took my mother by it the next day, so she could see it.

The moment we walked in she told me it was beautiful, but something very wrong was going on in the house. I had not told her of our experiences on the stairs or the upstairs. As we got near the stairs to see the bedrooms upstairs, she told me not to buy the house. She did not want to go upstairs. She told me something awful had happened on those stairs and in the bedrooms. She did go upstairs with me to see it but complained of the coldness on the stairway and also felt the same thing we had experienced in the one bedroom. She told me not to buy it.

My husband and I still wanted it and decided all the paranormal feelings were just crazy thoughts, although I was a little scared. We signed the papers anyway to buy it and had settled for a closing date just a week away. The very next day, we learned that the credit of the people who were buying our house fell through at the last minute, so we were not able to buy the house on S. Detroit. My mother always felt it was a godsend, that the house was haunted by evil and would have brought us sadness. I believe she was right.

Submitted by Anonymous, Xenia, Ohio

. . . .

6168540R00129

Printed in Great Britain
by Amazon.co.uk, Ltd.,
Marston Gate.